*"We should have every path laid open to woman
as freely as to man."*

—Margaret Fuller

Published by The Curious Traveller Press,
a division of The Pressroom, Inc., Gloucester, MA

1999 © Boston Women's Heritage Trail
Second Edition
ISBN 1-892839-03-2

Written by:
Polly Welts Kaufman, Bonnie Hurd Smith,
Mary Howland Smoyer, Susan Wilson

Special assistance from:
Jean Gibran, Sylvia McDowell

Interns:
Jody Noack, Katie Wright, Simmons College

Book design: Bonnie Hurd Smith

Logo design: Ginny O'Neil (see BB25)

Contemporary photography:
Joanne Ciccarello, Susan Wilson

First edition 1991 by Polly Welts Kaufman, Patricia Morris, and
Joyce Stevens, under a grant to the Boston Public Schools from
the Women's Educational Equity Act.

Cover
Background: photo by Joanne Ciccarello; Back Cover: photo
by Linda Haas; Front Cover: upper left (Anne Hutchinson statue)
photo by Susan Wilson; upper right (Phillis Wheatley), courtesy
of The Bostonian Society/Old State House; lower left (Amelia Earhart)
courtesy of The Schlesinger Library, Radcliffe College; lower right
(*Unity and Community* Mural, detail) photo by Susan Wilson.

Inside front cover
Upper left (Lucy Stone), photo by Susan Wilson; upper right (Josephine
St. Pierre Ruffin) courtesy of the Afro American Studies Center, Boston
University; lower left (Amy Beach), courtesy of Virginia Eskin; lower right
(Julia O'Connor [Parker]) courtesy of the International Brotherhood of
Electrical Workers.

Inside back cover
Upper left Jennie Loitman Barron) courtesy of The Schlesinger Library,
Radcliffe College; upper right (Muriel S. Snowden) photo by Judith Sedwick,
courtesy of Ben Wallace; lower right (Clementine Poto Langone) courtesy
of the Langone family; lower right (Mother Mary Joseph Rogers) courtesy of
the Maryknoll Mission Archives.

Boston Women's Heritage Trail

Four Centuries of Boston Women

A Guide to Five Walks

Downtown

North End

Beacon Hill

South Cove/Chinatown

Back Bay

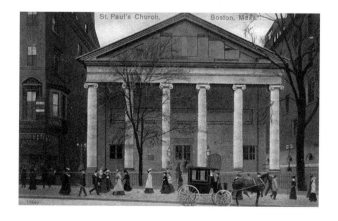

Boston Women's Heritage Trail
Boston, Massachusetts, 1999

M = historic marker at this site

Introduction

by Susan Wilson

"Remember the Ladies," wrote Abigail Adams to husband John in 1776, "and be more generous and favorable to them than your ancestors!" In the two centuries since Abigail's oft-quoted note, however, neither John nor the generations of men that followed did much to remember, credit, or commemorate the numerous women who helped mold and maintain the New Republic. Even in Boston, the acknowledged "Cradle of Liberty," the accomplishments of women were generally footnotes and afterthoughts, rather than the stuff of biographies, annual celebrations, and public statues.

In 1989 that all began to change, when a group of Boston Public School teachers, librarians, and their students brainstormed and inaugurated the *Boston Women's Heritage Trail*. Like The Hub's two extant walks— the *Freedom Trail* and the *Black Heritage Trail*—this new historic trek promised to take visitors through fascinating slices and stories from Boston's illustrious past. Unlike its predecessors, the *Boston Women's Heritage Trail* highlighted the work of women, from household names like Abigail Adams, Phillis Wheatley, Amelia Earhart, Louisa May Alcott, and Rose Kennedy, to less-familiar leaders like Chew Shee Chin, Julia O'Connor, Clementine Langone, and Melnea Cass.

Between 1989 and 1998, both scholarly research and schoolroom projects throughout the city added more women's names and historic sites to the original four-part trail. New routes were developed, and a variety of images were collected, enhancing the stories of women's lives with engaging visuals. The result is this updated, expanded, and illustrated guide to almost four centuries of women's accomplishments in The Hub.

So what's left to do?

The answer is simple: read, walk, share, enjoy. And with a little luck, we will all "remember the ladies" a bit better each time we follow in their footsteps and wander these historic paths.

> *"How...would New England's rocky soil and icy hills have been made mines of wealth unless there had been human beings born to oppose, delighting to combat and wrestle, and with an unconquerable power of will."*
> —Harriet Beecher Stowe

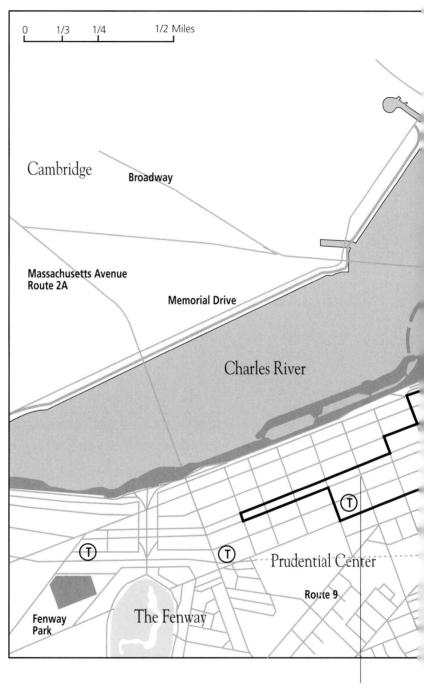

Boston, Massachusetts

0   1/3   1/4   1/2 Miles

Cambridge   **Broadway**

**Massachusetts Avenue
Route 2A**

Memorial Drive

Charles River

**Fenway
Park**

The Fenway

Prudential Center

Route 9

Back Bay Walk
page 50

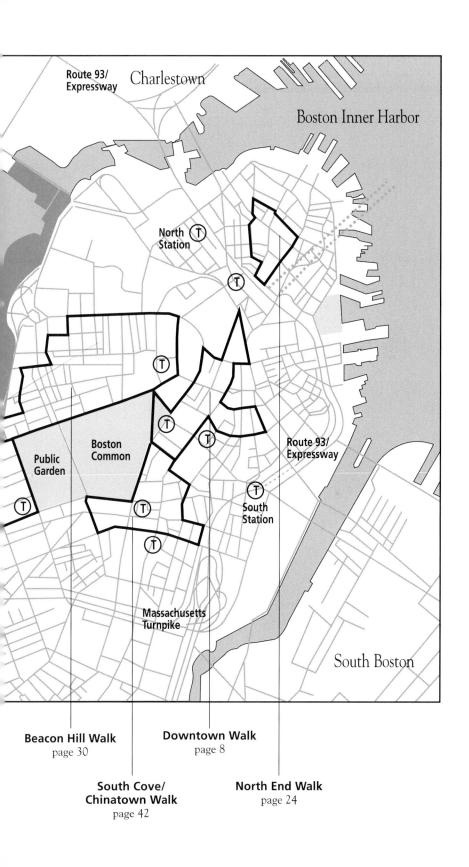

Route 93/
Expressway

Charlestown

Boston Inner Harbor

North
Station Ⓣ

Ⓣ

Ⓣ

Public
Garden

Boston
Common

Ⓣ

Ⓣ

Ⓣ

Route 93/
Expressway

Ⓣ

Ⓣ
South
Station

Ⓣ

Ⓣ

Massachusetts
Turnpike

South Boston

Beacon Hill Walk
page 30

Downtown Walk
page 8

**South Cove/
Chinatown Walk**
page 42

North End Walk
page 24

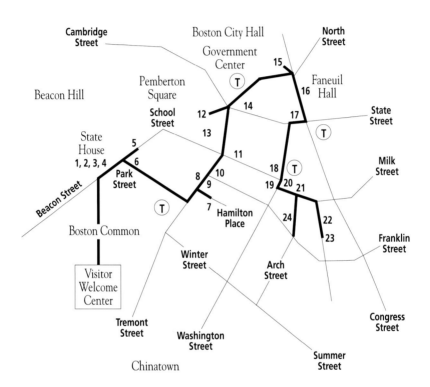

North End

Cambridge Street

Boston City Hall

North Street

Government Center

Beacon Hill

Pemberton Square

Faneuil Hall

State Street

School Street

State House

Milk Street

Park Street

Hamilton Place

Franklin Street

Boston Common

Winter Street

Arch Street

Visitor Welcome Center

Congress Street

Tremont Street

Washington Street

Summer Street

Chinatown

Downtown Walk
Use this map for all "D" sites

(T) = MBTA stop

⇜ Downtown Walk ⇝
The Search for Equal Rights

Beginning with Boston women who risked their lives for freedom
of religion in the 17th century, the Downtown Walk includes women
who spoke out for the abolition of slavery, female education,
woman suffrage, and Native American rights.

Time: 1 1/2 hours.
Begins: Visitor Welcome Center, Boston Common.
Directions: Walk up the hill, through the Common, to the State House.

> *"Now if you do condemn me for speaking what in
> my conscience I know to be the truth I must commit
> myself unto the Lord...."* —Anne Hutchinson

D1: Anne Hutchinson Statue
State House, Front of West Wing
Anne Hutchinson (1591-1643) was banished from Boston in the first decade
of settlement because her religious views were different from those of the
ruling ministers. Believing that both men and women could receive grace
only from God, she accused the ministers of preaching that "good works"
signified holiness. Hutchinson attracted women to prayer meetings she held
in her home in part because her beliefs put women's souls on an equal footing
with men's souls. She was a respected midwife and wife of an established
merchant, but was banished in 1638 for heresy (see also D17). This statue,
erected in 1922 as a gift of the Anne Hutchinson Memorial Association and
the State Federation of Women's Clubs, was sculpted by Cyrus E. Dallin.

D2: Mary Dyer Statue
State House, Front of East Wing
Mary Dyer (died 1660) was a Quaker whose doctrine
of Inner Light was similar to Hutchinson's salvation
by grace received directly from God. At the time,
practice of the Quaker religion was not allowed in
Massachusetts. She witnessed for religious freedom in
Boston three times. Twice she was banished, but the
third time she was hanged on Boston Common. Dyer
was a friend of Anne Hutchinson and walked out of
church beside her following Hutchinson's
excommunication. This statue, erected in 1959 from
a descendant's bequest, was sculpted by Sylvia
Shaw Judson.

Mary Dyer

D3: Nurses Hall and Gallery

State House, Second Floor

The statue of a Civil War nurse administering aid to a wounded soldier was a gift of the Massachusetts Daughters of Veterans in 1914. They called the nurses "Angels of Mercy and Life Amid Scenes of Conflict and Death." Louisa May Alcott (1832-1888), author of *Little Women*, served as a Civil War nurse in Georgetown, D.C., until she contracted typhoid fever. She wrote about her experiences in *Hospital Sketches* (see also B6). On the facing balcony wall is a painting honoring mothers of war by Boston artist Edward Brodney. His mother, Sarah Brodney, was the model for the central figure.

In 1996, the Massachusetts legislature recognized that the State House art collection included only a handful of images of women. They recommended that a new work of art be created to honor the contributions of women to public life in Massachusetts. Now permanently installed on a large wall just outside Doric Hall, the work depicts six women selected by an advisory committee. Dorothea L. Dix (1802-1887) (see D4), Florence Hope Luscomb (1887-1985) (see B17); Sarah Parker Remond (1826-1894) (see D13); Mary Kenney O'Sullivan (1864-1843) (see C9); Josephine St. Pierre Ruffin (1842-1924) (see B13); and Lucy Stone (1818-1893) (see D6) were chosen to represent all the women who dedicated themselves to improving life in the Commonwealth. The two-toned marble panels designed by artists Sheila Levrant de Bretteville and Susan Sellers include words written by the women etched on the stone and bronze busts cast from period photographs. Historical sources are used to reveal the personal and political challenges these women faced in their struggles to bring about social change.

D4: Dorothea Dix, House Chamber and Committee Rooms

State House, Third Floor

Dorothea Dix

Women were considered citizens with the right to petition long before they gained the right to vote in 1920. Abolitionist Angelina Grimké (1805-1879), who was raised by a slave-holding family in the South, spoke out against slavery on a tour of New England with her sister Sarah in 1837. In 1838, she presented a women's anti-slavery petition with 20,000 signatures to a committee of the state legislature and became the first woman to publicly address the legislature. In 1843, after an 18-month survey of jails and poorhouses in Massachusetts, Dorothea Dix (1802-1887) prepared a *Memorial* for the state legislature. "I come to place before the legislature of Massachusetts the condition of the miserable, the desolate, the outcast," Dix began, as she charged extreme cruelty in the treatment of the mentally ill. The state appropriated funds to improve one facility and she continued her investigations in many other states. During the Civil War, Dix was the superintendent of army nurses for the Union.

Directions: At the bottom of the State House steps, turn left on Beacon Street.

D5: The Boston Athenæum

10 1/2 Beacon Street

Many women played a role in the history of The Boston Athenæum, a library supported by memberships and thought to be the oldest library in America. Poet and celebrity Amy Lowell (1874-1925) was the first woman to be appointed to the Board of Directors. As a girl, Lowell had free run of the Athenæum. In 1903 when the trustees threatened to tear down the building, Amy Lowell led the protest. Her poetry flourished when, during a sojourn in Paris, she discovered French symbolism as expressed in the branch of poetry called "Imagism." She edited works of poetry as well as bringing out collections of her own work.

The Boston Athenæum's
Fifth Floor Reading Room

The Athenæum's art collection includes: *Puck and Owl*, a sculpture by Harriet Hosmer (1830-1908); a portrait of Hannah Adams (1755-1831), a scholar who was the first woman to be given reading privileges at the library; and a portrait by John Singer Sargent of Annie Adams Fields (1834-1915). Fields, a noted writer, poet, and social philanthropist, conducted a literary salon at her home at 148 Charles Street for the authors published by her husband's firm, Ticknor & Fields (see D17). In her will, she left $40,000 to Associated Charities of Boston.

Directions: Return to Park Street noting the monument to the 54th African American Civil War regiment and its leader, Robert Gould Shaw, by sculptor Augustus St. Gaudens.

> *"We, the people of the United States. Which 'We the people'? The women were not included."*
> —Lucy Stone

D6: *Woman's Journal* and 9 to 5 Office Workers' Union

5 Park Street

The offices of the *Woman's Journal,* the newspaper published by the American Woman Suffrage Association and the New England Women's Club, one of the first clubs for women in the country, were in another building on this site. Edited by Lucy Stone (1818-1893), the *Journal* chose office space as close to the seat of

The *Woman's Journal* office at 5 Park Street, c.1880

power—the State House—as possible. Stone petitioned annually for woman suffrage. In 1879 she testified: "In this very State House, how often have women looked down from the gallery while our law-makers voted down our rights, and heard them say, 'Half an hour is time enough to waste on it,'...[and then] turn eagerly to consider such a question as what shall be the size of a barrel of cranberries...[taking] plenty of time to consider that." Stone had been the first Massachusetts woman to receive a college degree when she graduated from Oberlin College in 1847. When she married Henry Blackwell she became the first married woman to officially keep her maiden

Lucy Stone

name, leading to the late 19th-century coining of the term "a Lucy Stoner" to mean a woman who stood up for her rights. Alice Stone Blackwell (1857-1950), Stone's daughter, edited the *Journal* in a building on Copley Square (see BB6) for 25 years until suffrage was granted in 1920.

In 1973, a trade union for women office workers named "9 to 5" held its first monthly meetings in this building now owned by the Paulist Fathers. A member decided to organize after her boss walked into the office and said, "Well, I guess there's no one here." 9 to 5 now meets at 145 Tremont Street and shares space with Local 925 of the Services Employees Union.

Directions: Continue down Park Street. Cross Tremont Street to Hamilton Place.

"If we ask ourselves Why is the subject of dress of such consequence? I think the answer will follow, Because a comparatively unimportant and external thing has come to stand as of the very first importance to the great majority of women...It was...painful to hear a devout woman, of years and wide experience say, 'I believe that the majority of women, if entering heaven to-day, would ask, not 'Where is my Lord?' but 'What do they wear there?'"
—Abby May

D7: Dress Reform Parlors and Milliners
Hamilton Place

The short streets running between Tremont and Washington streets— including Hamilton Place, Winter Street, and Temple Place— contained shops for women in the late 19th and early 20th centuries. Many women were successful proprietors of dressmaking and millinery shops, including Irish-born Ellen Hartnett, who rose from being a millinery worker in 1860 to a shop owner with capital 25 years later. In order to secure the best class of customers, some dressmakers, like Josephine McCluskey, took on new names— she became "Miss Delavenue." The area also supported Dress Reform Parlors in the 1880s, where women could be freed from the restrictive fashions of the day. They could purchase or buy patterns for such items as the "emancipation waist."

Directions: Return to Tremont Street and cross it again.

D8: Abiah Franklin and "Mother Goose"
Granary Burying Ground
Abiah Franklin (1667-1752), mother of Benjamin Franklin, was honored by her famous son when he erected the central high granite obelisk in memory of his parents. She raised 13 children, including Benjamin and Jane Franklin Mecom (see D20) and was called "a discreet and virtuous woman." Tradition states that Elizabeth Foster Vergoose, known as "Mother Goose," is buried here. Widowed, she lived with her eldest daughter and entertained her grandchildren with nursery rhymes. Her son-in-law, printer Thomas Fleet, reportedly published them as *Songs for the Nursery* or *Mother Goose's Melodies*.

Directions: Look across the street.

D9: Edmonia Lewis Studio
corner of Bromfield and Tremont Streets
(now Suffolk University Law School)
The studio of Edmonia Lewis (1845-c.1909), a member of the colony of women sculptors in Rome gathering around Charlotte Cushman in the mid-19th century (see N7), was located in a former building at this site from 1863-1865. As a child, Lewis, who had both African American and Chippewa ancestry, lived with her Chippewa mother's people. Although she was born free, her favorite subject for her sculpture was freedom from slavery, demonstrated in *Forever Free*, a sculpture depicting a man and woman breaking their chains, made as a tribute to abolitionist William Lloyd Garrison. It is now on display at the Howard University Gallery of Art. Her most popular work was a bust of Colonel Robert Gould Shaw, the white commander of the African American 54th Massachusetts Infantry during the Civil War. Lewis's identification with her Chippewa heritage caused her also to revere and create a bust of Henry Wadsworth Longfellow, author of the poem, *Hiawatha*. The sculpture is now owned by the Fogg Art Museum at Harvard University.

Edmonia Lewis

D10: Mary Baker Eddy and Tremont Temple
88 Tremont Street
In an earlier building on this site, 19th century women held many meetings urging the abolition of slavery, adoption of woman suffrage, and temperance reform. Here, in March 1885, Mary Baker Eddy (1821-1910), founder of the Church of Christ, Scientist, was given ten minutes to respond to a barrage of criticism from members of the Boston clergy. Her ideas about God as father-mother and of man and woman as co-equals— both created in God's image—

angered the ministers of the time. Her book, *Science and Health*, was a best seller. In the years following her talk, Eddy emerged as one of the most important women reformers of her day, pioneering in the field of mind-body medicine. Soon after she spoke in Tremont Temple, she wrote, "Let it not be heard in Boston that woman...has no rights which man is bound to respect....This is woman's hour, with all its sweet amenities and its moral and religious reforms."

Directions: Continue along Tremont Street. Turn right on School Street.

Mary Baker Eddy

D11: Boston School Committeewomen
Old City Hall, 45 School Street

Women were elected to the Boston School Committee before they could vote. In 1875, after a drive by the New England Women's Club, six women took their seats on the Boston School Committee elected by Boston men. Although the Committee was reduced from 116 to 24 members the following year, four women were reelected including Lucretia Crocker (1829-1886), who later became the first woman supervisor in the Boston Public Schools, and Abby May (1829-1888). May succeeded in starting a separate Latin School for girls, but it was not until 1972 that the two Latin schools became co-educational. When May was defeated for reelection, women all over Massachusetts petitioned the legislature and won the right to vote for school board members, starting in 1879.

Julia Harrington Duff (1859-1932) of Charlestown, a former Boston School teacher, was the first Irish-American woman to be elected to the Boston School Committee in 1900. Her rallying cry, "Boston schools for Boston girls," expressed her belief that Yankee teachers from outside the city were being hired in preference to the young Catholic women graduates of Boston's Normal School. Boston women teachers pressed for their rights. Among the women challenging the 1880s School Committee regulation that women resign upon marriage were Grace Lonergan Lorch (1903-1974) and Suzanne Revaleon Green. Green's husband, a lawyer, succeeded in having his wife and two other married teachers reinstated to their teaching positions. The regulation remained on the books, however, until 1953 when a state law required its removal.

Julia Harrington Duff

"The married teacher should 'stay at home and look after her household duties...." —Boston School Committeeman, quoted in the *Woman's Journal*, 1895.

Directions: Return to and cross Tremont Street.
Turn right. Go up the stairs through Center Plaza
to Pemberton Square. On your left is D12.

D12: Women Judges

Municipal Court House, Pemberton Square
Jennie Loitman Barron (1891-1969) became the
state's first full-time woman judge in 1934. She served
for thirty years, twenty in the Boston Municipal Court
and ten in the Superior Court. As a lawyer
representing the League of Women Voters, she
successfully argued for women's service on juries.
Before she became a judge, Barron served on the
Boston School Committee in the late 1920s, where
she focused attention on substandard school
conditions. In 2002, three out of ten of the Boston
Municipal Court justices are women.

Jennie Loitman Barron

Directions: Look to the right of the Court House
for the former location of the Howard Athenæum.

Sarah Parker Remond

D13: Sarah Parker Remond and the Howard Athenæum

Pemberton Square (formerly Scollay Square)
Sarah Parker Remond, the grand-
daughter of a free black who fought in
the American Revolution, committed
her first act of public resistance at the
Howard Athenæum. In 1853, Remond,
who lived in Salem, had purchased
tickets by mail for a performance at the
Howard. When she arrived, the theater
would not seat her in the seats she had
paid for but, instead, made her sit in the
segregated gallery. She refused,
departed, and later sued the theater,
winning $500 in damages. Remond
went on to become an international
anti-slavery lecturer.

The Howard Athenæum was opened
in 1846 with the first cushioned theater
seats in Boston. It was a fashionable
theater, playing opera and drama until
1870 when it turned to vaudeville. The
building was demolished in 1962.

Walk down the steps through Center Plaza
to Cambridge Street.

D14: Abigail Adams, Mercy Otis Warren, and Brattle Square

City Hall Plaza, Cambridge Street

Abigail Adams

The Boston City Hall Plaza covers the same ground as the 18th century Brattle Square. From 1768 to 1771, Abigail Adams (1744-1817) lived in two locations in and near Brattle Square with her husband, attorney John Adams, and their family. It was a period of increasing family responsibilities for her. Her five children were born between 1765 and 1772. The family lived there during the Boston Massacre, which took place nearby—just outside the Old State House—in 1770. After John Adams successfully defended the British soldiers involved in the incident, his health declined. The family moved back to their farm in Braintree (now Quincy) the following year, but returned to Boston in 1772. They were in Boston during the Boston Tea Party in 1773, but by 1774 the Adamses had moved back to the farm permanently because John began traveling for the new republic—first as a delegate to the Continental Congress in Philadelphia. Abigail Adams became well known as a critical thinker and correspondent with her husband, who was away from the farm for much of the next ten years. She managed the farm, their large family, and their financial affairs. Among her correspondents was philosopher and writer Mercy Otis Warren (1728-1814), who published in 1805 a three-volume history of the American Revolution.

"If peace and unanimity are cherished, and the equalization of liberty, and the equity and energy of law, maintained by harmony and justice, the present representative government may stand for ages a luminous monument of republican wisdom, virtue and integrity. The principles of the revolution ought ever to be the pole-star of the statesman...not only for the benefit of existing society, but with an eye to that fidelity which is due posterity."
—Mercy Otis Warren

Mercy Otis Warren

Directions: Walk down the City Hall Plaza steps and cross Congress Street to Faneuil Hall. Turn left. Cross North Street and into Carmen Park, between Congress and Union Streets.

D15: Holocaust Memorial
Carmen Park

Dozens of prominent Boston women were involved in planning and funding the New England Holocaust Memorial, some of them survivors of Nazi concentration camps who have found new lives in Boston. The Memorial was dedicated in October 1995 to foster the memory of, and reflection on, one of the great tragedies of modern times. The Memorial features six luminous glass towers etched with six million numbers to remind visitors of those who perished during the Holocaust, or *Shoah,* from 1933-1945. In total, the Memorial honors all eleven million people who perished because of their race, religion, nationality, physical disability or sexual preference, as well as those who courageously aided death camp survivors. The Memorial's dedication includes the words, "...know that wherever prejudice, discrimination and victimization are tolerated, evil like the Holocaust can happen again."

Directions: Return to Faneuil Hall. Note the statue of patriot Sam Adams by sculptor Anne Whitney (see B16).

D16: Protest Meetings and Faneuil Hall
Quincy Market

Faneuil Hall and the adjoining Quincy Market are the historic locations of Boston's great women's fairs and protest meetings. The Anti-Slavery Bazaars, sponsored by the Female Anti-Slavery Societies, were held there in the 1830s and 1840s. In September 1840, women held a seven-day fair to raise money to complete the building of the Bunker Hill monument. Inspired by Sarah Josepha Hale (1820-1879), the women raised $30,000 (see N4). Among the women's suffrage meetings held in Faneuil Hall was a New England Woman's Tea Party, sponsored on the centennial of the Boston Tea Party by the New England Woman Suffrage Association. They invited the public to join them in the celebration, noting that women were still subject to "taxation without representation."

Suzette "Bright Eyes" LaFleshe

Suzette "Bright Eyes" LaFleshe (1854-1903), an Omaha Indian, inspired the Indian Rights Movement when she spoke in Faneuil Hall in December 1879. LaFlesche, wearing native dress and a bear-claw necklace, protested the reservation system: "Did our Creator...intend that men created in his own image should be ruled over by another set of his creatures?" After hearing Bright Eyes speak in Boston, many Boston women became her supporters. Helen Hunt Jackson (1830-1885) was inspired by her speech to write *A Century of Dishonor,* a book that cited injustices to the Indian peoples that she gave to every member of the U.S. Congress.

Working women saw Faneuil Hall as a place for a forum for their demands. In 1903, the Women's Trade Union League was founded in Faneuil Hall (see C12). Massachusetts nurses also chose the hall to rally for professional status in 1903 when they founded the Massachusetts Nurses Association. Among the organizers was Lucy Lincoln Drown (1847-1934), superintendent of nurses at Boston City Hospital from 1885 to 1910. In 1919, the call for the women telephone operators' strike brought two thousand angry women to the hall (see C3).

Directions: Continue up Congress Street. Turn right on State Street noting the Old State House and the National Park Service Visitor Center. Turn left on Washington Street.

D17: Elizabeth Murray,
Corn Hill and Queen Street
(now, roughly, Court and Washington Streets)
Born in Scotland, Elizabeth Murray (1726-1785) came to Boston in 1749. At age 23 she established a business selling imported cloth and dry goods from Great Britain. She proved to be such a resourceful business woman that she soon earned enough money to be entirely self-sufficient—a rare achievement for a colonial woman. Although she married three times, Murray remained childless. Still, she oversaw the education and upbringing of her nieces, kindling in them a spirit of self-reliance and self-esteem. She helped them and other needy women set up shops of their own. Murray once wrote to a friend, "I'd rather [be] a useful member of society than all of the fine delicate creatures of the age."

> *"I'd rather [be] a useful member of society than all of the fine delicate creatures of the age."*
> —Elizabeth Murray

Directions: Continue on Washington Street. A plaque in Spring Lane, on the left, marks the site of the home of Mary Chilton Winslow (d.1679), a Mayflower passenger in1620. (see BB15)

D18: Old Corner Bookstore
corner of School and Washington Streets
(now the Boston Globe Store)
Anne Hutchinson lived in a house on this site in the mid 1630s across from Governor John Winthrop. It was here that she conducted women's prayer meetings (see D1). In the mid-19th century, the present building, known as the Old Corner Bookstore, housed the publishing firm of Ticknor and Fields. Annie Adams Fields (1834-1915), wife of publisher James T. Fields, conducted a literary salon for authors in the Fields' home on Charles Street. Annie Fields (see also D5) supported the work of many women writers, including Sarah Orne Jewett (1849-1909), poet Louise Imogen Guiney

Old Corner Bookstore building

(see BB9), and Harriet Beecher Stowe (1811-1896). Fields was also active in charitable works. She spent many hours at the Charity House on Chardon Street and cofounded the Cooperative Society of Visitors, a case review agency that made recommendations to the central administration of Boston's relief organizations for aid disbursement. The Society was absorbed into the Associated Charities of Boston. Fields's book *How to Help the Poor* served as an unofficial guide to the programs and policies of Associated Charities.

Irish Famine Memorial (detail)

D19: Irish Famine Memorial and Annie Sullivan

Corner of School and Washington Streets
The Irish Famine Memorial was dedicated in 1998 to commemorate the 150th anniversary of the Irish potato famine. It honors the arrival of Irish immigrants to Boston and their contributions to the city. Created by sculptor Robert Shure, the sculptures depict a starving family in Ireland begging for help, and one arriving in America. Among the Irish women honored by the *Boston Women's Heritage Trail* is Annie Sullivan Macy (1866-1936), known as the gifted teacher of Helen Keller. Born to poor Irish immigrants to Massachusetts, Sullivan progressively became blind. After the death of her mother and her father's abandonment, she entered an orphanage. In 1880, a supervisor placed

Annie Sullivan (left) and Helen Keller

"Children require guidance and sympathy far more than instruction."
—Annie Sullivan

her in the Perkins School for the Blind in South Boston. Two operations improved her eyesight enough so she could read, and Sullivan graduated as valedictorian of her class. She became the teacher of Helen Keller (1880-1968), who came from an advantaged family but could not hear, see, or speak. Sullivan devoted her life to Keller, who became a national celebrity, and saw Keller through her education and early career.

D20: Old South Meeting House and Phillis Wheatley

310 Washington Street

When Old South, the site of mass protest meetings in Revolutionary Boston, was slated for demolition a hundred years later, a group of women bought the building (but not the land) to protect it. Philanthropist Mary Tileston Hemenway (1820-1894) then contributed more than half the sum needed to preserve it, becoming an early leader in historic preservation.

Phillis Wheatley

Phillis Wheatley (c.1753-1784), the first African American poet to be published in book form, was a member of Old South. While still a child, she was purchased as a slave by the Wheatley family. Her poetry reflects her love of freedom: "Should you...wonder from whence my love of Freedom sprung...I, young in life, was snatched from Afric's fancy'd happy seat...such, such my case. And can I then but pray Others may never feel tyrannic sway?" An exhibit depicting her life is permanently displayed here. For the site marking Wheatley's landing place, see C5.

Directions: Turn left on Milk Street.

"Poetry is the voice through which I speak to the world. I was taken from my parents ...at the age of seven, my only memory being one of my mother pouring out water before the sun rose. That was in 1761, when I was transported as a slave to Boston...."
—Phillis Wheatley

D21: Birthplace of Jane Franklin Mecom

(and Benjamin Franklin), 17 Milk Street

Jane Franklin Mecom (1712-1794), Benjamin Franklin's sister and favorite family correspondent, survived the trials of raising nine children and many grandchildren in 18th-century Boston. After Mecom's husband died in 1765, she opened a boarding house near the Old State House, where legislators stayed frequently and kept her informed about local and national political issues. At the age of 76 she wrote: "I have a good clean House to live in...I go to bed Early lye warm & comfortable Rise Early to a good Fire have my Brakfast directly and Eate it with a good Apetite and then read or Work...we live frugaly Bake all our own Bread...a Friend sitts and chats a litle in the Evening...."

Birthplace of Jane Franklin Mecom

Directions: Continue down Milk Street to Federal Street.

D22: Susanna Rowson and Federal Street Theatre
Federal Street

Susanna Haswell Rowson (1760-1824), a playwright and an actress at the Federal Street Theater, was the author of the first American best-selling novel, *Charlotte Temple, A Tale of Truth*. Rowson arrived in America when she was six, but her father was a Loyalist and during the Revolution they were returned to England. Not long after her marriage to William Rowson, Susanna returned to America and settled in Boston where they both acted at the Federal Street Theatre. For the five years following 1796, she performed 129 different parts in 126 productions, many of which she wrote herself. Her next venture was to set up a Young Ladies Academy in 1797 near the theater. Rowson moved the school out of Boston but later returned. Her academy was one of the first to offer girls education above the elementary level and included instruction in music and public speaking.

Original cover of the novel, *Charlotte Temple*

Another woman playwright whose plays were performed at the Federal Street Theatre in 1795 and 1796 was Judith Sargent Murray (see D24). Her satirical plays, The *Medium or Happy Tea-Party* (later renamed *The Medium, or Virtue Triumphant*) and *The Traveller Returned*, addressed class structure and gender roles in the new republic.

Federal Street Theatre c.1795

D23: Federal Street Church
100 Federal Street

Among the more well-known Boston women who attended William Ellery Channing's Federal Street Church were abolitionists Maria Weston Chapman (1806-1885) and Eliza Lee Cabot Follen. Chapman, a founder of the Boston Female Anti-Slavery Society, was a supporter of abolitionist William Lloyd Garrison, publisher of the famed abolitionist newspaper

"A piercing voice of grief and wrong,/Goes upward from the groaning earth!/ Oh true and holy Lord! how long?/In majesty and might come forth!"
—Maria Weston Chapman, from *Songs of the Free*

> *"Mothers in the free states, I tell you no idle dream; I present no visionary impracticable idea. I tell you the simple truth, when I say you can, if you will, abolish slavery. The tender heart of the boy is in the hands of the mother."*
>
> —Eliza Follen, from the anti-slavery tract *To Mothers in Free States*

The Liberator. An inspired organizer and fundraiser, Chapman ran 22 yearly anti-slavery fairs in Boston beginning in 1834. One of her colleagues in this venture was Lydia Maria Child whose 1833 publication, *An Appeal in Behalf of that Class of Americans called Africans*, was the first book to advocate an immediate end to slavery. Chapman's fairs became a model for women in other parts of the country to raise money for the abolitionist cause. Chapman also published several important anti-slavery tracts including *How Can I Help Abolish Slavery?* and *Right and Wrong in Massachusetts.* With Garrison, Maria Chapman supported women's full participation in abolitionist work—including public speaking, which had been condemned in a pastoral letter from the Congregational ministers of Massachusetts as being outside women's God-ordained sphere. In 1840, Chapman was elected to the executive committee of the American Anti-Slavery Society.

Eliza Lee Cabot Follen (1787-1860) was best known for her anti-slavery writings including *Anti-Slavery Hymns and Songs* and *A Letter to Mothers in Free States.* In *A Letter*, Follen wrote, "...what can women,—what can we mothers do?...you can do everything; I repeat, you can abolish slavery. Let every mother take the subject to heart, as one in which she has a personal concern. In the silence of the night, let her listen to the slave-mothers crying to her for help...." Much of Follen's writing was designed for children, including songs, poems, and stories that carried a moral lesson.

Directions: Return to Milk Street and follow it back up to Arch Street. Turn left on Arch and walk to Franklin Street.

D24: Franklin Place and Home of Judith Sargent Murray

Franklin and Arch Streets

The Tontine Crescent was a fashionable place to live in the late 18th and early 19th-century Boston. The long row of elegant townhouses, designed by Boston architect Charles Bulfinch, was built in 1793 and named Franklin Place after Benjamin Franklin.

Franklin Place, The Tontine Crescent

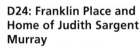

With the opening of the Back Bay for settlement, they declined in fashion and were demolished in 1872 after the Great Fire. Franklin Street still retains the curve of the buildings.

Among the notable women who lived there was Judith Sargent Murray (1751-1820), a native of Gloucester, who moved with her husband, John Murray, to No. 5 Franklin Place in 1794 (see N11). Judith Sargent Murray was already a successful writer, publishing a regular column in the *Massachusetts Magazine*, a new literary monthly, titled "The Gleaner." Using a male persona, she expressed her opinions on female equality, education, federalism, and republicanism. She wrote that not only should a woman be educated to be "the sensible and informed" companion of men, but she should also be equipped to earn her own living. Murray saw the many new female academies as inaugurating "a new era in female history." In 1798, she published her "Gleaner" essays in a book she also called *The Gleaner*, selling it to a list of subscribers headed by George Washington. *The Gleaner* became a minor classic, and Murray became the first woman in America to self-publish. She was also a poet and published in various Boston periodicals under the pen names "Honora Martesia" and "Constantia." An avid letter writer, the copies of letters Murray wrote from 1765-1818 (ages 14-67) were discovered in 1984, and offer a new eyewitness account of early American history.

Judith Sargent Stevens (Murray)

Abby May (1829-1888), also an advocate for women's rights, lived at 5 Franklin Place with her family as a young woman. Among her many achievements, May succeeded in starting a separate Latin Schoool for girls and served as one of the first women on the Boston School Committee (see D7 and D11).

Directions: Continue up Franklin Street to Washington Street. If you turn left on Washington Street to West Street, you can join the Chinatown loop of the Boston Women's Heritage Trail. If you turn left on Washington Street and right on Winter Street, you will arrive at the Boston Common near Park Street below the State House, where you started the Downtown Walk.

"The idea of the incapability of women is...totally inadmissible.... To argue against facts, is indeed contending with both wind and tide; and, borne down by accumulating examples, conviction of the utility of the present plans will pervade the public mind, and not a dissenting voice will be heard."
—Judith Sargent Murray

End of Walk.

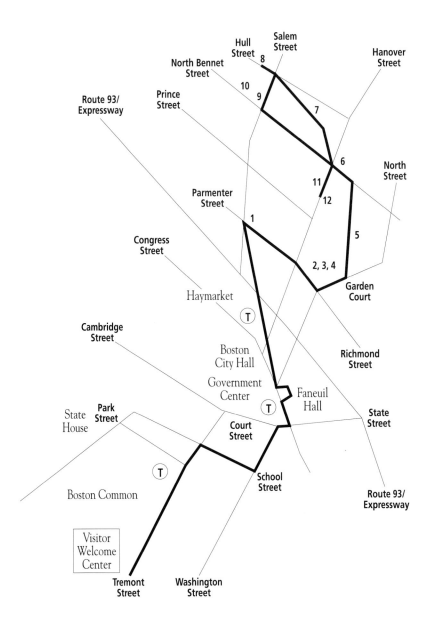

North End Walk
Use this map for all "N" sites

(T) = MBTA stop

➢ North End Walk ➢
A Diversity of Cultures

The North End Walk presents the lives of women from the variety of ethnic groups who have lived in the North End. Beginning with Yankee women active in support of the American Revolution, the walk continues with the activities of the Irish, Jewish, and Italian women who made the North End their first home in Boston.

Time: 1 1/2 hours.
Begins: National Park Service Visitor Center, 15 State Street.
Directions: Follow the *Freedom Trail's* red line north to Faneuil Hall, turning left on Congress Street. Walk north, toward the North End, crossing under the Expressway, until you reach Salem Street in the North End. Continue to Parmenter Street and turn right.

N1: North End Union
20 Parmenter Street
Helping to meet the needs of Irish, Jewish, and Italian immigrant families was the goal of the North End Union which was founded in 1892. It is still an important community center. In 1976, North End women made the Bicentennial quilt now on display in Hubbard Hall to celebrate the history of their neighborhood. Boston's first public playground, a sand garden, was started by a committee of philanthropic women in the yard of the Chapel that occupied the site in 1886 (see plaque). "Playing in the dirt is the royalty of

Children in the North End Union's sandbox, c.1886

"Playing in the dirt is the royalty of childhood."
—Kate Gannett Wells

childhood," said committee member Kate Gannett Wells (1838-1911). Mothers supervised children at first; later, employed kindergarten teachers read to the children and taught them crafts and led them in marching and singing. Across the street is the North End Branch of the Boston Public Library, built on the site of the Charlotte Cushman School (named for the renowned 19th-century actress who was born in a house on that site in 1816 (see N7)). Inside is a diorama of the Ducal Palace in Venice made by artist Louise Stimson (1890-1981) in 1949 (see BB9).

Clementine Poto Langone

Directions: Cross Hanover Street to Richmond Street. Turn left on North Street, bearing left to North Square.

N2: Poto Family Grocery Store

33 North Square

The former home and grocery store of the family of Clementine Poto Langone (1898-1964) is now a coffee shop. As a child, she helped pack Italian food products to send west to Italian immigrants working on the transcontinental railroads. The grocery store was on the first floor with living quarters upstairs. When Clementine married Joseph Langone, Jr. in 1920, she moved next door to 190 North Street. In the 1930s, after her husband was elected to public office, she helped many Italian immigrants become citizens so they could be eligible for social security benefits and provided food and clothing to Italian people out of work. She was an active member of the North End Union.

N3: Home of Rachel and Paul Revere

19 North Square

When she became Rachel Walker Revere (1745-1813) by marrying the recently-widowed Paul Revere in 1773, Rachel took on the care of the six surviving children born to Paul's first wife, Sarah Orne Revere (1736-1773), who died four months after her eighth child was born. Rachel had eight more children, three of whom did not reach maturity. Large families and a high infant mortality rate were common during colonial times. In 1775, Rachel held the family and business together when the British did not allow Revere to return to Boston after his famous ride. She eventually joined him in Watertown until they returned to their home after the British evacuated Boston on March 17, 1776. Across the street is Rachel Revere Park, first dedicated in 1946 and restored at the time of the Bicentennial in July 1976.

Interior, Paul Revere House

N4: Mariners House

11 North Square

Sarah Josepha Hale (1788-1879), editor of Boston's *Ladies' Magazine*, established the Seaman's Aid Society in 1833 to provide employment for the wives of sailors as seamstresses and a place to sell their work. The Society also opened a Mariners House in the North End as a sailors' boarding house and developed an industrial school for seamen's daughters and a day nursery. Hale later became the editor of *Godey's Lady's Book*. In September of 1840, Hale organized the great women's fair which raised enough money to complete the Bunker Hill monument. It had stood unfinished for more than a decade (see D15).

Directions: Continue straight ahead to Garden Court.

N5: Rose Fitzgerald Kennedy Birthplace

Sarah Josepha Hale

4 Garden Court

The birthplace of Rose Fitzgerald Kennedy (1890-1995), daughter of John F. Fitzgerald, who became the first Boston-born Irish-American mayor in 1905, and mother of President John F. Kennedy and Attorney General Robert Kennedy, probably was a bow fronted building like the one at No. 6 Garden Court. Rose Kennedy devoted her life to raising her nine children and was active in special education as well as in her sons' political campaigns.

Directions: Turn left to Hanover Street, and then turn right.

N6: Old St. Stephen's Church

401 Hanover Street

The only remaining church in Boston designed by architect Charles Bulfinch was completed in 1804. Its history reflects the neighborhood. In 1862, it became a Roman Catholic Church and Rose Fitzgerald Kennedy and her father were christened here. On the pews are the names of the North End women and men who helped raise the funds for the church's restoration in 1965. A marker in memory of Rose Kennedy commemorates her baptism (see N5).

Directions: Cross over Hanover Street to Revere Mall. Follow the wall on the left.

Rose Kennedy, with Joe Jr.

N7: Plaques to North End Women

Revere Mall

Three women prominent in North End history are honored by plaques on the left wall of Revere Mall. At the age of ten, Ann Pollard (1620-1725) was probably the first white woman to come ashore in Boston, landing with Governor John Winthrop at the foot of today's Prince Street. Dr. Harriot Keziah Hunt (1805-1875), who grew up on the waterfront at the foot of Hanover Street, became a doctor through self-study after being refused permission to attend lectures at Harvard Medical School. A women's rights advocate and social reformer, Hunt advocated health education for women. Charlotte Cushman (1816-1876), who was born on the site of the present North End branch library, became an internationally-known actress renowned for playing both male and female roles. She established a salon in Rome for women sculptors including Boston sculptors Anne Whitney (see B16) and Edmonia Lewis (see D9) and Watertown's Harriet Hosmer.

Directions: Cross Salem Street to Hull Street directly opposite the Old North Church.

Charlotte Cushman, in the 1860s, as a Shakespearean character

Samples of the highly collectible pottery

N8: Paul Revere Pottery and Library Clubhouse
18 Hull Street

The first home of the Paul Revere Pottery, founded in 1908 by librarian Edith Guerrier (1870-1958) and artist Edith Brown (1872-1932) and funded by philanthropist Helen Osborne Storrow (1864-1944), was in the basement of this building. Reflecting the philosophy of the Arts and Crafts movement, the pottery provided worthwhile employment for young North End Italian and Jewish women. The lower floors of the building served as the Library Club House under the supervision of Guerrier, where young women formed clubs for reading, storytelling, and dramatics named for their meeting times. The Saturday Evening Girls continued to meet until 1969. The Pottery moved to Nottingham Hill in Brighton in 1915, operating until 1942.

Members of the Saturday Evening Girls' Club and associated Library Clubs decorating pieces of Paul Revere Pottery at 18 Hull Street c.1912

Directions: Return to Salem Street and turn right.

N9: North Bennet Street Industrial School
Corner of Salem Street

Pauline Agassiz Shaw (1841-1917) founded the North Bennet Street Industrial School in 1881 to train newly arrived Italian and Jewish people in skilled trades. America's first trade school, the school now holds an international reputation for courses in fine furniture, jewelry, violin making, carpentry,

and piano and violin restoration. Shaw, active in social reform, gave financial support to the woman suffrage movement. She is also responsible for the institutionalization of kindergartens in Boston Public Schools. In the 1880s, she developed kindergartens in fourteen schools using her own funds and energy. In 1887, the School Committee accepted responsibility for continuing those kindergartens, gradually adding more.

N10: Hebrew Industrial School
Baldwin Place

Pauline Agassiz Shaw

One of the locations of the Hebrew Industrial School, founded for girls in 1889, was next to the North Bennet Street Industrial School. It was later named for Jewish activist Lina Hecht (1848-1920). At a time when nearly a third of the North End's population was Jewish, the school was established to train Jewish women in needlework skills. Anxious to teach their own youth, the Hebrew Ladies' Sewing Society donated cloth and sewing machines for classes in millinery, hand sewing, power sewing, and pattern cutting. The school became Hecht Neighborhood House in 1922 in a different place and moved to Dorchester in 1936 where it served the community for another thirty years.

Directions: Return to North Bennet Street. Turn right on Hanover Street.

N11: Universalist Meeting House
332 Hanover Street (now the North End Community Center)

Writer Judith Sargent Murray, an advocate for women's equality, attended Boston's first Universalist meeting house at this site when she moved to Boston in 1794 (see D24). Her husband, John Murray, an early Universalist preacher, served here as pastor from 1793 until 1809 when he suffered a stroke. Among the progressive ideas preached here was the equality of male and female souls—not unlike views espoused years earlier by Anne Hutchinson (see D1) and Mary Dyer (see D2). In her writing, Murray used her theological knowledge to challenge the legitimacy of the centuries-old "Fall of Eve" myth and its damaging effect on views about women.

Directions: Continue down Hanover Street.

N12: St. Leonard's Church
Hanover Street, between North Bennet and Prince Streets

St. Leonard's Church was the first Roman Catholic Church founded by Italian immigrants in Boston. Built in 1873, St. Leonard's was restored in 1988. Women were prominent in the drive which raised more than a million dollars for the project. Their names are included on the tablets in the church's Peace Garden.

Directions: Return to Salem Street and walk south towards Faneuil Hall.

End of Walk.

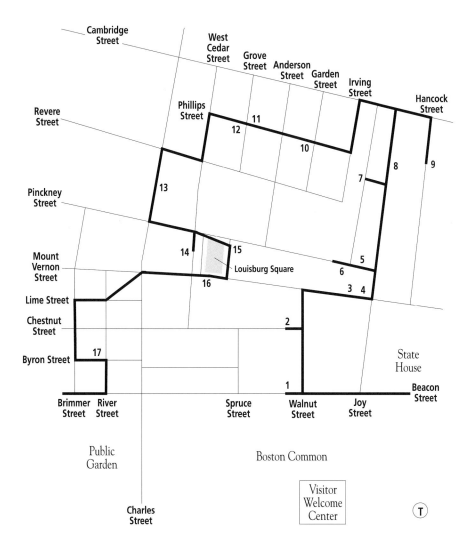

Beacon Hill Walk
Use this map for all "B" sites

(T) = MBTA stop

☞ Beacon Hill Walk ☜

Writers, Artists, and Activists

Women writers and artists living on Beacon Hill used their talents
to support social movements ranging from anti-slavery to peace.
The walk also tells the story of African American women who
were abolitionists, one who became a renowned sculptor, and
another who became the first African American registered nurse.

Time: 1 1/2 hours.
Begins: The State House.
Directions: Walk down Beacon Street, away from Park Street.

B1: Women's City Club

40 Beacon Street
Founded in 1914 by a group of women headed by Helen Osborne Storrow
(1864-1944) as a service club for women, the Women's City Club membership
rose to 5,000 by the mid-1920s. Storrow also brought Girl Scouts to Boston
and sponsored girls' clubs and the Paul Revere Pottery which provided
employment for young women (see N8). The Women's City Club sold its
building in 1992 and now shares its space with the Union Club.

*Directions: Walk back up Beacon Street to
Walnut Street, the first left. Walk up Walnut
Street to Chestnut Street. Turn left.*

> *"It is a new world today. I find
> it filled with a new hope and
> brightened by a new inspiration."*
> —Julia Ward Howe

B2: Home of Julia Ward Howe

13 Chestnut Street
Best known as the author of *The Battle
Hymn of the Republic*, written at the
beginning of the Civil War, Julia Ward
Howe (1819-1910) lived here during that
period, one of her several different
residences in Boston. Howe was a noted
reformer and early participant in the
women's club movement after the war. She
was joined by a group of women, including
Caroline Severance (1820-1914), in
founding the New England Women's Club
in 1868, one of the first women's clubs in
the country. She followed Severance as

Julia Ward Howe

The houses owned by Hebzibah Clarke Swan

president. Howe was a leader in the suffrage movement and helped found the *Woman's Journal*. In 1872, she initiated the first Mother's Day, characterizing it as a Day for Peace. Howe read papers at the meetings of the Radical Club, a club for women and men who were "daring thinkers," which met at this site from 1867-1880 (see D6). The house was designed by Charles Bulfinch c.1806 and was one of three adjoining houses Hebzibah Clarke Swan (1757-1825) gave as wedding presents to her three daughters. Swan was one of five original proprietors of Beacon Hill at a time when it was rare for a woman to own property in her own name.

Directions: Return to Walnut Street and turn left.
Turn right on Mount Vernon Street.

B3: Rose Nichols and Nichols House Museum
55 Mount Vernon Street
Rose Standish Nichols (1872-1964) was among the first well-known women landscape architects and a lifelong pacifist who lived on Mount Vernon Street her entire life. She traveled extensively throughout the world and developed an interest in international politics. She left her house to the public and as a place for offices of organizations promoting international friendship.

Directions: Continue up Mount Vernon Street.

B4: Portia School of Law
45-47 Mount Vernon Street
Portia School of Law began in 1908 when two women who wanted to take the Massachusetts bar examination asked Attorney Arthur W. MacLean to tutor them. His wife Bertha named the nascent school after Portia who disguises herself as a lawyer in Shakespeare's *Merchant of Venice*. The informal school expanded and

A class in legal history at
Portia School of Law, c. 1940

became the only school providing legal education for women exclusively. Portia Law was incorporated in 1919 and in 1920 the first L.L.B. degrees were awarded to 39 women. The school continued to grow, admitting a few men in 1930. The first woman dean was Margaret H. Bauer (1899-1985), who served in various capacities at the school from 1937 until 1962, becoming dean in 1952. In June 1972, the name of the school was changed to the New England School of Law. It moved to 154 Stuart Street in 1980.

In 1923, Blanche Woodson Braxton (1894-1939), a graduate of Portia Law in 1921, became the first African American woman to be admitted to the Massachusetts Bar. She later became the first African American woman admitted to practice in the U.S. District Court in the state. The first woman president of the Board of Trustees of New England School of Law was Anna E. Hirsch (1902-1997), a 1928 graduate of Portia Law. Hirsch was elected register of probate for Norfolk County in 1954 and again in 1960 (see also C2).

Directions: Continue up Mount Vernon Street. Turn left down Joy Street to Pinckney Street. Turn left.

B5: Elizabeth Peabody's Kindergarten
15 Pinckney Street
One of the locations for the kindergarten of Elizabeth Palmer Peabody (1804-1894) (see C1), considered the founder of the kindergarten movement in the United States, was at 15 Pinckney Street which, although destroyed, was the mirror image of 17 Pinckney Street. Influenced by the ideas of Friedrich Froebel, Peabody became an advocate for kindergartens nationwide, publishing the *Kindergarten Messenger* and organizing the American Froebel Union. She was a link between the visionaries of the Transcendental movement and educational reforms.

Elizabeth Palmer Peabody

> *"My mother said,*
> *'Every child should*
> *be taught as if he or*
> *she were a genius.'"*
> —Elizabeth Peabody

B6: Home of Louisa May Alcott
20 Pinckney Street
Although author Louisa May Alcott (1832-1888) is best known for her book, *Little Women*, describing her family life in Concord, Massachusetts, she had several Boston homes. The daughter of famed Transcendentalist Bronson Alcott, she lived here in rented rooms as a child. As an adult, she often stayed with other

Louisa May Alcott

> *"So hard to move people out of old ruts. I haven't patience enough. If they won't see and work, I let 'em alone and steam along my own way."*
> —Louisa May Alcott

reformist women in the "sky parlor" of the Bellevue Hotel on Beacon Street, owned by Dr. Dio Lewis, principal of Boston's Normal Institute for Physical Education, and near her publisher, Roberts Brothers. In the last decade of her life, Alcott purchased a home for her family at 10 Louisburg Square, but was too ill to enjoy it for herself. She died at the age of 55, probably of poison from the mercury used to treat the typhoid fever she contracted as a Civil War nurse (see D3).

Directions: Return to Joy Street and turn left. Enter Smith Court.

B7: African Meeting House
8 Smith Court (now also the Museum of Afro American History)
Among women abolitionists active in this church before the Civil War was Maria Stewart (1803-1879) who challenged other free African American women: "O, ye daughters of Africa, awake! Awake! Arise! No longer sleep nor slumber, but distinguish yourselves. Show forth to the world that ye are endowed with noble and exalted faculties." The church was built in 1805-1806 in the heart of Boston's African American community on the north slope of Beacon Hill.

Susan Paul (see B14), whose father was the minister, joined other African American women to form a temperance society in the 1830s. Escaped slaves William and Ellen Craft (1826-1897) were active in abolition meetings here (see B12). The Smith School, at the corner of Smith Court, was the impetus for Boston's first successful desegregation case in 1855.

The Museum of Afro American History, which was founded in 1964 by Sue Bailey Thurman (1903-1996), owns the Meeting House and is also located in Smith Court. Thurman's portrait hangs just inside the museum's main door.

> *"O, ye daughters of Africa! What have ye done to immortalize your names beyond the grave? What examples have ye set before the rising generation? What foundation have ye laid for the generations yet unborn? Where are our union and love? And where is our sympathy, that weeps at another's woe, and hides the faults we see?"*
> —Maria Stewart

Directions: Return to Joy Street and turn left.

African Meeting House/
Museum of Afro American History

B8: Home of Rebecca Lee Crumpler

67 Joy Street

Dr. Rebecca Lee Crumpler (1831-1895) is considered to be the first African American woman doctor. She received a "Doctress of Medicine" in 1864 from the New England Female Medical College in Boston's South End, later merged into the Boston University School of Medicine. Born in Delaware, Crumpler was raised in Pennsylvania by an aunt. She came to Charlestown in 1852 where she worked as a nurse. After she received her degree, she practiced in post Civil War Virginia. With her husband, Dr. Arthur Crumpler, she next moved back to Boston where she set up her medical practice on Joy Street. She focused on women and children and emphasized nutrition and preventive medicine. She pulled together her experiences and knowledge in *A Book of Medical Discourses in Two Parts*.

Directions: Continue down Joy Street, turning right on Cambridge Street. Turn right on Hancock Street.

B9: Home for Aged Colored Females

22 Hancock Street

Established on Beacon Hill in 1860 at the beginning of the Civil War by both African American and white abolitionists, the home provided old-age housing for women who were ex-slaves as well as for Black women from Boston's free Black community who had lived and worked in Boston. The home was moved to this site in 1901 and continued here into the 1920s.

Directions: Return to Cambridge Street. Turn left, passing Joy Street. Turn left on Irving Street, and right on Phillips Street.

B10: The Vilna Shul

14-18 Phillips Street

Now the Center for Jewish Heritage, the Vilna Shul was built in 1919 to serve the Jewish community on Beacon Hill as a synagogue and community center. Although it closed in 1985, the building is currently being restored as a Jewish cultural center. Before they built the synagogue, the congregation of Lithuanian Jews worshipped in temporary spaces for nearly 25 years. They named the synagogue for the city of Vilna, because they considered it to be the center of Jewish culture in Lithuania, the former home of many of the

"Ours is not the first generation to understand that Jewish women are part of Jewish history. But ours is the first generation with the resources— the wisdom, wealth, and passion—to systemically preserve the record of Jewish women's lives." —from a publication of the Jewish Women's Archive

Interior of The Vilna Shul

members. The names of the women who were among the founding members of the synagogue are listed in a plaque in the back of the sanctuary. Although the entire congregation sat on the same level, the women's section was separate from the men's section but equal in size (which was typical of synagogues of that time). The Vilna Shul is also a significant site because it represents the large Jewish community who made their first Boston homes in the old West End and on the north slope of Beacon Hill.

The Vilna Shul

B11: View of Massachusetts General Hospital: Linda Richards and Mary Eliza Mahoney

(from corner of Phillips and Grove Streets)

Linda Richards (1841-1930) pioneered professional nurses' training at Massachusetts General Hospital. In 1873 she had received the first diploma from the country's first nursing school which was organized at the New England Hospital for Women and Children. The hospital, founded in Roxbury in 1863 and run by Dr. Marie Zakrzewska (1829-1902) and a board of women reformers, is now the Dimock Community Health Center. The Palmer-Davis Library at Massachusetts

Linda Richards

General is named for Sophia Palmer (1853-1920) and Mary E.P. Davis (1840-1924), both students of Linda Richards. Palmer and Davis co-founded the *American Journal of Nursing* and created the American Nurses Association by bringing together alumnae associations of nurses' training schools.

"It was my determination to prove to the profession, as well as the laity, that a woman has not only the same (if not more) physical endurance than a man, while I thus created a good foundation of respect for women physicians." —Dr. Marie Zakrzewska

Mary Eliza Mahoney (1845-1926), the first African American woman to become a registered nurse, also graduated from the New England Hospital. Mahoney is honored by a medal awarded annually by the American Nurses Association. Mary Vincent (1818-1887) was an actress whose friends funded the Vincent Memorial Hospital, part of Massachusetts General, in her memory in 1891. The women of the Vincent Club continue to raise money by producing an annual theatrical show. The hospital pioneered in women's health, including the development of the "Pap Smear."

Directions: Continue along Phillips Street.

Mary Eliza Mahoney

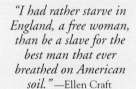

B12: Ellen and William Craft, home of Harriet and Lewis Hayden
66 Phillips Street

This station on the Underground Railroad was a destination for many fugitive slaves, including Ellen Craft (1826-1897) and her husband, William. In 1848 she disguised herself as her master, bandaged as if ill, and tended to by her husband as if he were the slave. They escaped from Georgia by taking the train and steamer to Boston. After two years in Boston where they were active in the anti-slavery cause, they sailed to England, staying until after the Civil War because the new Fugitive Slave Law endangered their lives. Harriet Hayden (c.1816-1893) and her husband, Lewis Hayden, both born slaves, owned this house for more than 40 years. Harriet Hayden bequeathed a scholarship for "needy and worthy colored students" at Harvard Medical School. Harriet and Lewis also worked with Underground Railroad "conductor" Harriet Tubman (c.1820-1913), called the "Moses of her People," who was known for moving slaves to safe havens. A statue of Harriet Tubman stands in Harriet Tubman Park in the South End.

Ellen Craft, in disguise

"I had rather starve in England, a free woman, than be a slave for the best man that ever breathed on American soil." —Ellen Craft

Directions: Continue along Phillips Street. Turn left on West Cedar Street. Turn right on Revere Street. Turn left on Charles Street.

"We need to talk over not only things which are of vital importance to us as women, but also things which are of especial importance as colored women...for the sake of our own dignity, the dignity of our race, and future good name of our children, it is...our...duty to stand forth and declare our principles, to teach our ignorant and suspicious world...our aims and interests."
—Josephine St. Pierre Ruffin

B13: Josephine St. Pierre Ruffin, Florida Ruffin Ridley, and *The Woman's Era Club*

103 Charles Street

Josephine St. Pierre Ruffin (1842-1924), African American editor and publisher of *The Woman's Era*, the journal of the New Era Club, lived here for two decades. She founded the club for African American women in 1894. A year later, she organized a national conference to form the National Federation of Afro-American Women to show the existence of a "large and growing class" of cultured African American women. They met at the Charles Street A.M.E. Church (now Meeting House) and merged with the Colored Women's League to form the National Association of Colored Women in 1896. Ruffin served as the first vice president. Although it was accepted by the Massachusetts State Federation of Womens' Clubs, the New Era Club was refused membership in the national federation in 1900 for fear of offending Southern members.

Florida Ruffin Ridley (1861-1943), Ruffin's daughter with her husband, George Ruffin, the first African American judge in the North, became the second African American teacher in the Boston Public Schools. She was active with her mother in the New Era Club as well as in the League for Community Service. She also

Josephine St. Pierre Ruffin

"Negroes have been identified with the history of Boston from the earliest days of the town, and even as slaves made outstanding contributions. Phyllis [sic.] Wheatley adds a compelling note to Boston's claim to literary distinction; her poems were published in London in 1733. Copp's Hill, the Granary, and King's Chapel Burying Ground all hold the bodies of Negroes who served in one way or another in American wars, beginning with the American Revolution."
—Florida Ruffin Ridley, in *The Negro in Boston*, 1927

became a member of several predominantly white clubs, including the Twentieth Century Club and the Women's City Club of Boston (see B1). In addition to her work as a club woman and civil rights activist, Ridley was an essayist and journalist, focusing much of her writing on race relations in New England. In the 1920s, her interest in history led her to found the Society of the Descendents of Early New England Negroes. Through this work, she hoped to connect an understanding of history with contemporary work for social justice. African Americans and whites have always been involved, she wrote, "in the eternal war for justice and liberty which the state has waged." Then, as in her own time, she believed both races deserved an equal place in society.

Directions: Continue along Charles Street to Pinckney Street. Turn left. Turn right on West Cedar Street.

B14: Home of Susan Paul

36 West Cedar Street

In the 1830s, Susan Paul (1809-1841) taught at the Smith School on Joy Street, a segregated school for African American children funded jointly by the city and private donations (see B7). Paul was also an officer in the Boston Female Anti-Slavery Society founded by Maria Weston Chapman in 1832 (see D22). She was the daughter of Thomas Paul, the founder of the African Baptist Church, and supported her mother after his death. Some of her letters were printed in William Lloyd Garrison's *Liberator*. In 1834 she wrote to condemn the "spirit which persecutes us on account of our color—that cruel prejudice which deprives us of every privilege whereby we might elevate ourselves—and then condemns us because we are not more refined and intelligent."

Directions: Return to Pinckney Street. Walk into Louisburg Square.

B15: St. Margaret's Convent

19 Louisburg Square

Originally founded in Sussex, England, in 1855 to care for the poor and ill in the surrounding countryside, this Episcopalian religious community came to Boston in 1873 to act as superintendents of a children's hospital. The sisters moved to three townhouses on Louisburg Square in 1883 which they used as a convent, chapel, and small hospital. Here, they expanded their nursing and evangelical

Interior of St. Margaret's Convent in 1990

teachings to reach the sick and poor on Beacon Hill and its environs. They ran St. Monica's Home, a nursing home for Black women and children, on Joy Street and later in Roxbury until 1988. In 1992, the St. Margaret's community moved the Motherhouse to Roxbury.

Directions: Walk through Louisburg Square to Mount Vernon Street. On your way, note 10 Louisburg Square, the last residence of Louisa May Alcott.

10 Louisburg Square, the last residence of Louisa May Alcott

B16: Anne Whitney Studio
92 Mount Vernon Street

The window on the top of this building marked the studio for two decades of sculptor Anne Whitney (1821-1915), who was part of a group of American women sculptors gathering around actress Charlotte Cushman in Rome in the mid-19th century (see N7). In 1873, soon after Whitney returned to Boston, she received a commission for the statue of Sam Adams now standing outside Faneuil Hall. Her statue of Leif Ericsson is on the Commonwealth Avenue mall (see BB25). Her bust of Lucy Stone is in the Boston Public Library (see BB9), and her sculpture of abolitionist William Lloyd Garrison is in the Massachusetts Historical Society. Whitney had a "Boston marriage" with her longtime companion Adeline Manning. During the late Victorian era, such marriages between women, generally professional and upper class, were both common and accepted by society at large.

Directions: Go down Mount Vernon Street. Cross Charles Street, noting the Charles Street Meeting House at the corner (see B13). Turn left on River Street. Turn right on Lime Street. Note the arts and crafts building at 26-28 Lime Street where jewelers and metalsmiths who were members of the Society of Arts and Crafts (see BB11) had their studios. Turn left on Brimmer Street. Turn left on Byron Street.

Anne Whitney (seated) with Adeline Manning

B17: Women's International League for Peace and Freedom: Florence Hope Luscomb and Emily Greene Balch

6 Byron Street

Between World Wars I and II, 6 Byron Street was the office of the Massachusetts Women's International League for Peace and Freedom. Florence Luscomb (1887-1985) was executive secretary of the office from 1929-1933. An early graduate of MIT, Luscomb gave up her career in architecture to work full time for the women's movement. After suffrage was passed, she was the executive secretary for the newly formed Massachusetts League of Women Voters and narrowly missed being elected to the Boston City Council. She became involved in the labor movement and ran for governor in 1952, continuing her antiwar and civil rights activities until her death. During the time the WILPF office was here, Emily Greene Balch (1867-1961), the second American woman to earn the Nobel Peace Prize, served as national president. Balch was a native of Boston and a former Wellesley College professor. From

Florence Hope Luscomb selling the *Woman's Journal*

1919 to 1922, as first international secretary-treasurer of WILPF in Geneva, Balch launched the new organization and set up its guidelines. In 1946, Balch followed Jane Addams (1860-1935) when she earned the Nobel Peace Prize in recognition of her efforts and the work of WILPF.

Emily Greene Balch

"I see no possibilities of social progress apart from fundamental changes on both the economic and the political side...Peace is too small a word for this."
—Emily Greene Balch

Directions: Continue on Byron Street. Turn right on River Street. Turn left on Beacon Street. You can pick up the Back Bay Walk at this point. (See page 48.)

End of Walk.

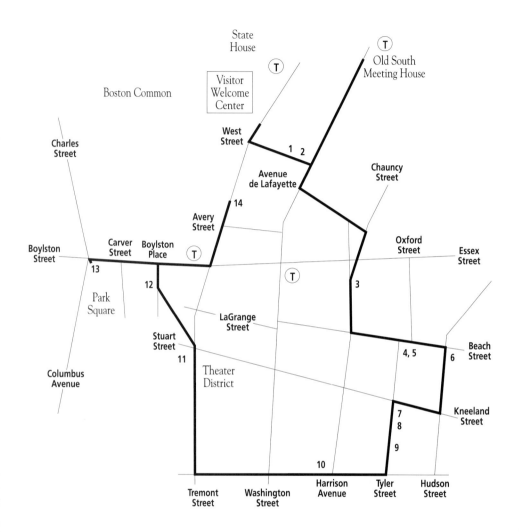

South Cove/Chinatown Walk

Use this map for all "C" sites

(T) = MBTA stop

☙ South Cove/Chinatown Walk ❧
Action for Economic and Social Justice

Women's organizations working for social change and economic
equality are described in the South Cove/Chinatown Walk.
Ranging from women's trade union activities to the international
programs of a Catholic sisterhood, the walk includes the story of
a woman-run settlement house and a famous cooking school.

Time: 1 1/2 hours.
Begins: Visitor Welcome Center, Boston Common,
or Old South Meeting House, 308 Washington Street.
Directions: From the Welcome Center, cross Tremont Street,
turn left on West Street. From Old South Meeting House,
walk south on Washington Street. Turn right on West Street.
For Old South, see D19.

C1: Elizabeth Peabody Book Shop
13-15 West Street

The Book Shop of Elizabeth Peabody (1804-1894) is best
known as the location of the 1839-44 Conversations led
by Margaret Fuller (1810-1850) which helped crystallize
New England Transcendentalism, a movement
encouraging the perfection of each individual. A regular
participant in these Conversations was philosopher and
activist Edna Dow Littlehale Cheney (1824-1904) who,
at age 16, was the youngest participant (see also BB3).
Fuller received an intense classical education from her
father and became known as an intellectual prodigy.
Working with Ralph Waldo Emerson and others, she
edited the transcendentalist journal *The Dial* and was the
first woman journalist for the *New York Tribune*. Her essay
Woman in the Nineteenth Century is an American feminist
classic.

Margaret Fuller

Elizabeth Peabody, also a Transcendentalist, founded
American kindergartens (see B5) and here at the Book
Shop became the first woman publisher in Boston. Her
younger sisters were each married in the family parlor
behind the Book Shop. Sophia (1809-1871), an artist,

*"...men are called on from an early period to reproduce all that they learn.
Their college exercises, their political duties, their professional studies...call on
them to put to use what they have learned. But women learn without any
attempt to reproduce. Their only reproduction is for purposes of display. It is to
supply this defect that these conversations have been planned."* —Margaret Fuller

married author Nathaniel Hawthorne, and Mary (1806-1887), an educator, married Horace Mann, considered to be the father of American public education.

C2: Massachusetts Bar Association
20 West Street
The first woman member of the Massachusetts Bar Association was Mary A. Mahan of West Roxbury, who was admitted in 1913. Many women lawyers in Boston attended Portia School of Law, established in 1908 (see B4). After Mahan was admitted along with with 34 men, a member spoke up saying he hoped her admission would "not interfere with our banquets and prevent smoking," but, he added, showing his pride in their action, " the question of women members has been brought before the American Bar Association and the members have dodged it."

Directions: Walk down to Washington Street and turn right. Turn left on Avenue de Lafayette and right on Chauncy Street to Harrison Avenue.

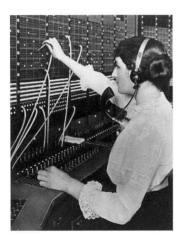

A woman telephone operator at New England Telephone c.1926

C3: Telephone Exchange
2-8 Harrison Avenue and Oxford Place
A successful and nonviolent strike of 8,000 women telephone operators in April 1919, led by Julia O'Connor [Parker] (1890-1972), paralyzed telephone service in five New England states for six days. This building is an expansion of the Oxford Street exchange where O'Connor worked. Switchboard operators, who were mostly young single Irish-American women, were expected to work at breakneck speed often on split shifts. They were punished with detention as if they were still in high school. Supported by the Women's Trade Union League, O'Connor and her team negotiated a settlement that included a $3 to $4 weekly raise (see C12). Starting in 1939, O'Connor worked for 18 years as an organizer for the AFL.

Directions: Look across the street to the second story window and note the sign for the International Ladies Garment Workers Union. Below the telephone building, continue on Harrison Avenue. Turn left on Beach Street. Stop at the corner of Beach and Tyler Streets. South and east of Beach Street was South Cove, a tidal flat until the 1830s.

Women telephone operators in 1919

C4: New England Chinese Women's Association
2 Tyler Street

The blue and gold sign on the second floor marks the New England Chinese Women's Association founded in 1942 by Chew Shee Chin (1899-1985) and other Boston Chinese women in response to Madame Chiang Kai Shek's appeal for China relief during World War II. The association continues to serve the Boston Chinese community as a networking and social service organization. Chew Shee Chin was one of the first Chinese-American women to work in Boston's garment industry (see C10).

Chew Shee Chin

C5: Phillis Wheatley Landing Place

Beach and Tyler Streets

Phillis Wheatley (c1753-1784), the first published African American woman poet in America, landed while still a small child in 1761 in the slave ship *Phillis* at Avery's Wharf located near the present position of Tyler Street. She was purchased at auction by the Wheatley family. Her mistress, Suzannah Wheatley, became her mentor (see also D20).

Directions: Return to Beach Street and turn left. Walk to the Chinatown Gateway Park on Hudson Street and turn right. In the park, note the Tianamin Memorial dedicated in 1989 to honor the 1989 Democracy Movement in China.

C6: Ruby Foo's Den
Beach and Hudson Streets (presently the site of Gateway Park)

Born in San Francisco, Ruby Foo (1904-1950) moved to Boston in 1923 where she began a single-room restaurant in Boston's Chinatown. Its popularity quickly grew, and she opened Ruby Foo's "Den" on Hudson Street in 1929—heralded as the first Chinese restaurant to successfully cater to non-Chinese clientele. Throughout World War II, the Den remained a legendary meeting place for theatrical and sports figures and other celebrities. She opened similar restaurants in New York, Miami, Washington and Providence, becoming a nationally-known restaurateur and mentor to dozens of aspiring chefs in her native Boston. In 1938, newspapers ran a photo of a Chinese baby sitting amidst rubble in a Shanghai railroad station that had been bombed by the

Ruby Foo's obituary in *The Boston Daily Globe*

FOO
Continued from the First Page

The thrice-married Mrs. Foo was one of Boston's most well-known figures for many years. Besides her famed "Den" on

RUBY FOO

Hudson st., she owned a part interest in a New York "Den."

Her elaborate Chinese restaurant here was known throughout the country and leading theatrical and sports figures flocked to taste the Chinese specialties.

Japanese. Foo had the child brought to the United States where she adopted him and raised him along with her other children.

Directions: Walk south along Hudson to Kneeland Street. Turn right. Turn left on Tyler Street.

C7: Lebanese-Syrian Ladies' Aid Society
76 Tyler Street

The women of the Lebanese-Syrian Ladies' Aid Society raised money for new arrivals and to provide relief during World War II to people in the Near East. Founded in the South Cove area in 1917, the society sponsored events for fundraising that made them a center for the social life of the community. It later moved to the South End.

C8: Maryknoll Sisters
79 Tyler Street

Mother Mary Joseph Rogers

"I love the expression 'the understanding of the heart.' It seems to me that understanding is the keynote of true love, just as misunderstadning is fertile soil for hatred." —Mother Mary Joseph Rogers

Mother Mary Joseph Rogers (1882-1955), a Boston Public School graduate and teacher, founded the Maryknoll Sisters of St. Dominic, a national order whose members were first known for their professional service in China before the Communist takeover. Rogers insisted that the sisters be trained professionally for their missionary work and that they work together as equals, sharing all household tasks. Under her leadership, over 1,000 women worked throughout the world in over 25 different countries spreading their message of Justice, Love and Peace in God's name, and living with and caring for those in need. The sisters still serve all over the world today, particularly in Latin America. The mission on Tyler Street served the Chinese community until 1992.

C9: Quincy School and Denison House
90 and 93 Tyler Street

When the innovative Quincy School opened in 1847, teachers had their own classrooms for the first time in America. Women teachers were in charge of each grade, but were supervised by a male principal. Students sat at their own desks instead of at long benches. Boys and girls attended different grammar schools; the Quincy School was for boys. Today, the

Mary Kenney O'Sullivan

Chinese-American Civic Association runs a multi-service center in the building.

Denison House, a woman-run settlement house, occupied three buildings across the street for 50 years (now a vacant lot). Founded in 1892 by the College Settlement House Association, Denison House was directed by Helena Dudley (1858-1932) and Vida Scudder (1861-1954), a Wellesley College professor. Their shop sold crafts produced by local women. They ran a medical dispensary, a milk station, and taught English. The

Denison House

heritage of Lebanese, Syrian, and Italian immigrant women was honored through crafts and folk dancing. Dudley believed women's greatest need was for a living wage and helped organize the Women's Trade Union League (see C12). When aviator Amelia Earhart (1897-1937) was a social worker there, she showered Boston with leaflets from a plane announcing a Denison House street fair.

After an earlier association with Chicago's settlement house, Hull House, labor organizer Mary Kenney O'Sullivan (1864-1943) worked for a time at Denison House. She lived there with her husband, John F. O'Sullivan, labor editor of *The Boston Globe*, and their three children. After his sudden death in 1902, she managed a model tenement and continued her labor organizing activities. She was one of the principal founders of the National Women's Trade Union League at Faneuil Hall in 1903 (see D15). O'Sullivan supported many union activities, including the 1912 Lawrence textile strike. She was a strong supporter of woman suffrage and opposed the entry of the United States into World War I, joining the Women's International League for Peace and Freedom. In 1914, she became a factory inspector under the Massachusetts Department of Labor and Industries.

Directions: Continue to the end of Tyler Street. Turn right on Oak Street.

C10: Chinatown Community Mural, *Unity and Community*
4 Oak Street
In this 40' mural, Chinese-American women are honored for their many roles in Asian-American community life. Designed by Wen-Ti Tsen and David Fichter in 1986, the colorful painting

Unity and Community Mural

shows a woman garment worker sewing a long piece of fabric which weaves through the composition and represents women's contribution to the cohesiveness of the community. Before the liberalization of immigration laws, fewer than twenty percent of Chinatown's residents were women.

Directions: As you continue along Oak Street, crossing Washington to Tremont Street, notice the friezes on the new Quincy School designed by artist Maria Termini, using drawings by children in the old Quincy School. Turn right on Tremont Street.

C11: Chinese Cultural Institute
276 Tremont Street
Art historian Doris C.J. Chu founded the art gallery of the Chinese Cultural Institute in 1980 to promote racial harmony through cultural understanding and to stimulate interest in Chinese history, philosophy, literature, and art. The Institute displays Chinese art and offers Chinese plays, concerts, lectures, and workshops. In 1998, the center opened a new theater with a play written by Chu called *That Gentleman from China*, based on a true story of Chinese immigration.

Julia O'Connor [Parker]

"We are just like soldiers patrolling in a just cause ...not one of us will flinch until we have won."
—Julia O'Connor [Parker]

Directions: Continue down Tremont Street passing the Wang Center and the Wilbur Theater, noting the Schubert Theater across the street. Both the Wilbur and the Schubert display plaques listing names of famous actresses who have performed on their stages. Cross Tremont Street at the corner of Stuart Street and cross Stuart Street to the Transportation Building on the left. Walk through the Atrium to Boylston Place.

C12: Boston Women's Trade Union League
5 Boylston Place
During the Great Depression, the Boston Women's Trade Union League maintained offices and a soup kitchen in this building owned and occupied on the upper floors by Boston's exclusive Tavern Club for men. Soon after the National WTUL was established at Faneuil Hall in 1903, the Boston branch assisted women workers in forming trade unions and aiding strikes, including the telephone operators' strike of 1919 (see C3). Although upper middle class women reformers began the BWTUL, women workers joined and held major offices. Among the presidents were telephone operators Julia O'Connor [Parker] (see C3) and Rose Finkelstein Norwood (1891-1980). For 50 years they also helped organize Boston library workers, retail clerks, and office cleaners.

Directions: Turn left on Boylston Street to Park Square.

C13: Women Editors
Park Square

Novelist Pauline Hopkins (1856-1930) edited *The Colored American* from 1900 to 1904 in an office at 5 Park Square. Her goal was to publish a journal devoted to "the development of Afro-American art and literature." She included a series of articles, *Famous Women of the Negro Race*, and reported the news of the rejection of Josephine St. Pierre Ruffin's New Era Club for membership in the General Federation of Women's Clubs in 1902 (see B13). Other publications edited by women with offices in Park Square include *Our Bodies Ourselves*, published by the Boston Women's Health Collective in 1970, and *Equal Times*, a newspaper for working women published in the mid-1970s and early 1980s. The Collective is located now in Somerville.

Directions: Go east on Boylston Street to Tremont. Turn left and continue along the Boston Common toward the Boston Common Visitor Welcome Center. When passing the Colonial Theatre, note the plaque listing prominent actresses who performed there.

> "Fiction is of great value to any people as a preserver of manners and customs...*No one will do this for us; we must ourselves develop the men and women who will faithfully portray the inmost thoughts and feelings of the Negro with all the fire and romance which lie dormant in our history,* and, as yet, unrecognized by writers of the Anglo-Saxon race."
> —Pauline E. Hopkins, from her 1900 book *Contending Forces, A Romance Illustrative of Negro Life North and South*

C14: Boston Cooking School
174 Tremont Street

As principal of the Boston Cooking School, the earliest women's school for professional cooking in Boston, Fannie Farmer published her famous cookbook from this site in 1896. Her cookbook revolutionized cooking by using scientific measurements in its recipes. Within 50 years, nearly three million copies were printed, making Fannie Farmer's name a household word. She hoped her book would "awaken an interest...which will lead to deeper thought and broader study of what to eat."

The Original Boston Cooking School Cook Book and Our Bodies Ourselves

Directions: Continue along Boston Common to the Visitor Center. If you want to join the Back Bay Walk (see page 50), return to Boylston Street and continue to the Women's Educational and Industrial Union at 356 Boylston Street.

End of Walk.

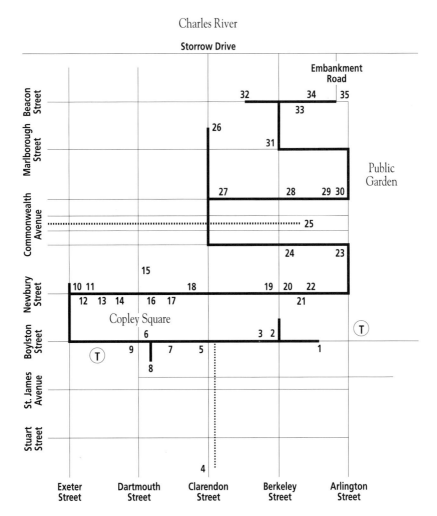

Back Bay Walk

Use this map for all "BB" sites

...... = this part of the walk optional

(T) = MBTA stop

☞ Back Bay Walk ☜

Educators, Artists, and Social Reformers

The Back Bay Walk begins with two sites devoted to supporting
rural and immigrant women who came to Boston during the city's
early growth. It continues by pointing out educational institutions,
clubs, and art associations, several founded by women to serve women.
The sites range from women's sculptures to mansions given by women
to educational and cultural institutions. They demonstrate the high
degree of energy devoted by Boston women to the arts and education.

Time: 1 1/2 hours
Begins: 356 Boylston Street, the first site.
Directions: From the Visitor Welcome Center on Boston Common,
walk along Tremont Street and turn right on Boylston Street.
The Women's Educational and Industrial Union, is on the left,
about four blocks down, under the golden swan.

Right: Artist Sarah Anne Rockwell created
four dioramas that tell the story of the
historical development of the Back Bay. They
are now displayed in the lobby of The New
England at 501 Boylston Street. Beginning as
an art student in the 1940s, Rockwell studied
diorama construction under Theodore Pitman
and continued after his death in 1956.
The New England dioramas took months of
research. Each element in the dioramas is in
perfect scale. A human figure took her two
weeks to complete and a horse, four weeks.
The replica of the Museum of Natural History
(see BB2) took her seven months to construct.
She worked from the original blueprints and
maintained the scale, beginning with each
brick and brownstone.

BB1: Women's Educational and Industrial Union

356 Boylston Street

The Women's Educational and Industrial
Union has served Boston women
continuously for nearly 125 years. It was
organized in response to the problems for
women and their families generated by
Boston's rapid urbanization and increased
immigration. The WEIU's first program was
a shop selling women's crafts and food, but

An accounting class at the Women's Educational
and Industrial Union, c.1940

Amelia Earhart, in the cockpit
of a training plane, 1926

*"...now and then women
should do for themselves
what men have already
done—and occasionally
what men have
not done—thereby
establishing themselves as
persons and encouraging
other women toward
greater independence of
thought and action."*
—Amelia Earhart

it rapidly moved into job training, placement, and protection of women workers. In recent years it instituted training for licensed home day care providers and created a transitional housing program for single mothers.

Dr. Harriet Clisby (1831-1931), an early woman doctor and women's rights activist from Australia, founded the WEIU in 1877 after calling together a group of prominent Bostonians including Julia Ward Howe (see B2), Louisa May Alcott (see B6), and Abby Morton Diaz (1821-1904). Diaz became president when Clisby left after three years to found a similar union in Geneva. Diaz saw the WEIU as a sisterhood for "both working girls in the cities and women of means," she said, because they shared a "universality of needs [which] places all on a kind of equality." The union gives an annual Amelia Earhart Award to honor an outstanding Boston woman. Before Earhart became famous as an aviator, the WEIU's career services department found her a position as a social worker at Denison House (see C9).

Bertha Mahoney Miller (1882-1969) ran the Bookshop for Boys and Girls at the union from 1916 to 1936, developing story hours and a traveling Book Caravan. Together with Elinor Whitney, she founded *The Horn Book Magazine* in 1924, the first journal devoted exclusively to children's literature.

A swan identifies the WEIU's present building because it was organized in 1877, the same year that the swan boats first sailed in the Public Garden.

Directions: Continue west along Boylston Street, noting the "Mama Bear" sculpture designed by Robert Shure at the FAO Schwartz toy store at Berkeley Street.

BB2: Museum of Natural History
234 Berkeley Street at Boylston
(now Louis of Boston)
At its founding in 1830, women were not allowed to become members of the Boston Society of Natural History which was at this site from 1864 to 1951, although they could use its

Interior of the Museum of Natural History
c.1900

resources. When the society sought to expand its membership in 1876, a great debate ensued. An opponent believed that "the presence of charming girls among the young students of science would be a great hindrance to any cold consideration of abstruse scientific thought." A proponent countered that women "would make as good members. . . and as interested an audience, as 9/10ths of the male members." Another supported the admission of women because they were "human beings even if they are of one sex."

Although fifteen women were soon admitted, women did not have a major influence until the society established a Teachers' School of Science in 1870. When support for the school lagged, Lucretia Crocker (1829-1886) (see D11), supervisor of science for the Boston Public Schools, and philanthropist Pauline Agassiz Shaw (1841-1917) (see N9), raised the necessary funds to continue it. Noting the progress women teachers made in the school, the Woman's Education Association sponsored summer classes for teachers at Annisquam, Massachusetts in 1881. This led to the establishment of the Marine Biological Laboratory at Woods Hole on Cape Cod a few years later. In 1951 the museum, renamed the Museum of Science, moved to Science Park on the Charles River.

BB3: Rogers Building, Massachusetts Institute of Technology

501 Boylston Street

Although she was not directly connected with the Rogers Building, known as "Tech on Boylston Street" from 1886 to 1916, Ellen Swallow Richards (1842-1911) holds an important role in the history of the Massachusetts Institute of Technology. When she was admitted as a special student in chemistry in 1870, she became the first woman to study at MIT. She was awarded a B.S. degree three years later, but the

Ellen Swallow Richards (left) testing the water at Jamaica Pond

doctorate for which she was qualified was refused her, it is believed, because the school did not want a woman to receive the first doctorate in chemistry. Richards, who pioneered the field of sanitary engineering and home economics, established a Woman's Laboratory at MIT in 1875 with funding from the Woman's Education Association. When her students were admitted to regular courses at MIT, Richards closed the laboratory and, aided by Ednah Dow Cheney (1824-1904), Lucretia Crocker (1829-1886), and Abby W. May (1829-1888) (see D11), established a parlor and reading room for women students in a new MIT building. It was dedicated to the memory of Cheney's daughter Margaret, a student at MIT who would have been the second woman graduate had she not died of typhoid fever in 1882. In that year, four women received regular degrees. Richards continued to be connected with MIT as an instructor and laboratory scientist in sanitary chemistry and engineering, and in connection with her pioneering studies of air, water and food, is said to have coined the word "ecology."

Directions: For the next site, either turn left and walk south down Clarendon Street or look left to identify the site. Afterwards, return to Boylston Street.

BB4: Young Women's Christian Association (YWCA)

140 Clarendon Street

The Boston Young Women's Christian Association, the first in the nation, was founded in 1866 by upper middle-class Protestant women. Led by Pauline Durant (1832-1917) until 1905, the YWCA hoped to guide and guard the young rural women coming to the city to work. The YWCA provided them with lodging and employment assistance. By the early 20th century, the YWCA had added a School of Domestic

Melnea Cass

Science and a popular gymnasium. The young women whom they served began to take an active role in the organization's management and established a busy club program. Confronting racism in the 1930s and 1940s, the YWCA integrated its branches and named Lucy Miller Mitchell as the first board member of color in 1941. Mitchell, who became executive director of Associated Day Care Services of Metropolitan Boston, was a local and national pioneer in the development of standards for child care.

The YWCA on Clarendon Street, with its popular swimming pool and increased residential facilities, was constructed in 1929. It is now named for Melnea Cass (1896-1978), a leader in increasing educational and occupational opportunities for African Americans. Known as "The First Lady of Roxbury," she was also a tireless activist for civil rights and a pioneer in the day care movement. The YWCA supports training for non-traditional careers and runs a child care center. It also operates a transitional housing space and job training at Aswalos House in Dorchester. Most recently, in 1998, it participated in opening the nation's first public housing facility for "grand families"—families consisting of grandparents raising their granchildren.

BB5: Sarah Wyman Whitman Window

Trinity Church Parish House, Copley Square

Artist Sarah Wyman Whitman (1842-1904) designed the stained glass window in the Trinity Church Parish House to commemorate the life of the Reverend Phillips Brooks, first rector of the church. A devoted member of the church, Whitman taught Sunday Bible classes for women for thirty years. Upon the death of Brooks in 1893, Whitman and her class campaigned for three years before she was allowed to create the window. A stained glass window across from Whitman's window is dedicated to her memory. In addition to fabricating stained glass, Whitman painted landscapes, flowers, and portraits and designed more than 200 book covers for the Boston publisher Houghton Mifflin.

Directions: Return to Boylston Street and continue west.

BB6: Massachusetts Woman Suffrage Association

Chauncy Hall, 585 Boylston Street

Chauncy Hall in 1913 was a "busy bee hive full of workers for women," according to the *Boston American* in 1913. It had housed the Massachusetts Woman Suffrage Association and the *Woman's Journal* since 1909 when they moved from 5 Park Street (see D6). In the last years of the suffrage campaign, the MWSA shared the building with the College Equal Suffrage Association, the Massachusetts Men's League for Woman Suffrage, the Boston Equal Suffrage Association for Good Government, and the New England Woman Suffrage Association. Women opponents to suffrage were not far. The Massachusetts Association Opposed to the Further Extension of Suffrage to Women had its office two blocks west, at the corner of Boylston and Exeter Streets. The group worked closely with the men's Massachusetts Anti-Suffragist Committee.

Boston Daily Globe,
August 19, 1920

Boston Daily Globe

WOMAN SUFFRAGE WINS AS TENNESSEE RATIFIES

Alice Stone Blackwell (1857-1950), daughter of Lucy Stone and Henry Blackwell, edited the *Woman's Journal* for 35 years after her graduation from Boston University in 1881. She served as president of the MWSA from 1910 until women achieved suffrage in 1920. In addition to helping start the League of Women Voters, successor to the MWSA, Blackwell was active in many other causes including relief for Armenian refugees, the Women's Trade Union League, the National Association for the Advancement of Colored People, and the American Peace Society. As a young valedictorian, she had predicted her life of dissent, saying, "It's perhaps the first, but I don't mean it to be the last, old fence I shall break through."

BB7: Boston Marathon Finish Line Tortoise and Hare Sculpture

Copley Square

In celebration of the 100th anniversary of the Boston Marathon in 1996, Nancy Schön, a former marathon runner, created the sculpture, *The Hare and the Tortoise*, at the finish line. Her *Make Way for Ducklings* statue is located in the Public Garden. Women were not allowed to enter the marathon as official runners until 1972 when Nina Kuscsik became the first female to be crowned with the laurel wreath. The first unofficial woman winner was Roberta Gibb in 1966. Joan Benoit Samuelson,

Joan Benoit Samuelson, winning in 1983

who in 1984 was awarded the gold medal in the first women's Olympic marathon, won the Boston Marathon in 1979 and 1983. Other women Olympic gold medal winners who also placed first in the Boston Marathon were Fatama Robba, Boston winner in 1997 and 1998, and Rosa Mota, Boston winner in 1987, 1988, and 1990.

Directions: Look left, down Dartmouth Street.

BB8: Hotel and Restaurant Workers' Union

Fairmont Copley Plaza Hotel, Copley Square

Until the mid-1960s, only male waiters could work in local hotels organized by the Greater Boston Hotel and Restaurant Workers' Union. At that time, 57 women waitresses, who were members of an all-women's union (Local 277) took their traveling cards to Local 34 of the union and asked for membership. When they were refused, the women sued. Supported by the Massachusetts Council Against Discrimination, the waitresses won their battle in June 1966. As members of the current local, Number 26, women now have the right to equal employment and equal pay in such union hotels as the Fairmont Copley Plaza, and are represented on the executive board of the union.

Directions: Return to Boylston and continue westward.

BB9: Boston Public Library

666 Boylston Street

The "BPL," as it is commonly known, has served as an intellectual and educational center for Boston women, from reformers to newly-arrived immigrants, since it opened in 1854. Housed in the elegant McKim building since 1895, the library was called a "noble treasure house of learning" by Russian immigrant, Mary Antin (1881-1949). She wrote, to be "in the midst of all the books that ever were written was a miracle as great as any on record." Many Boston women have also worked as library professionals including Louise Imogen Guiney (1861-1920), who later became a respected poet and writer and filled a role as an ambassador between the Irish Catholic community and the Boston Brahmins.

Lucy Stone,
by Anne Whitney

Women pioneered children's services at the library. Alice M. Jordan (1870-1960) was the first Supervisor of Work with Children, serving from 1900 to 1940. In 1906 she founded the New England Round Table of Children's Librarians to provide a meeting ground for this emerging profession. Since 1960, the round table and the Massachusetts Library Association have sponsored the Jordan-Miller Storytelling Program in recognition of Jordan's commitment to storytelling. Beryl Robinson (1906-1989), an African American, introduced storytelling to children in the BPL branches all over the city in the 1940s and 1950s. Her stories came from many cultures. In 1958-1959, she produced and told stories on public television, extending her audience to children throughout eastern Massachusetts.

Several women are included in the library's art collection. The Charlotte Cushman Room on the third floor of the McKim building is named for one of Boston's favorite 19th-century dramatic actresses and art patrons, who was born in the North End (see N7). A bust by Anne Whitney (see B16) of Lucy Stone (see D6), Boston suffragist and founder of the *Woman's Journal*, is displayed in the Main Reading Room.

Dioramas created by Louise Stimson (1890-1981) in the 1940s, also on the third floor of the McKim Building, depict miniature scenes of famous artists and their paintings.

Directions: Leave the library through the doors of the Philip Johnson addition, turning left on to Boylston Street. Turn right (north) from Boylston Street down Exeter Street to Newbury Street. On your left, note the Prince School, built as a Boston Public School in the 1870s.

BB10: Exeter Street Theater and Spiritual Temple
Corner of Exeter and Newbury Streets (now Waterstones Booksellers)
Though known as the Exeter Street Theater after 1913, this building was built as the First Spiritualist Temple in 1885. Young women played an important role in spiritualist meetings. They sometimes served on stage as mediums through whom it was believed a departed spirit was speaking. Two sisters, Viola and Florence Berlin, ran the Exeter Street Theater for many years, turning it into a popular place to see foreign films. The theater closed in 1984.

BB11: Society of Arts and Crafts
175 Newbury Street
Women were active in the Society of Arts and Crafts from its beginning. It was founded in 1897 as an expression of the Arts and Crafts Movement and is the oldest nonprofit craft organization in America. It encourages the creation and collection of the work of craft artists and awards an annual Medal of Excellence in Craft. Painter and art patron Sarah Choate Sears (see BB30) was a member of the original incorporating committee and, along with Sarah Wyman Whitman (see BB5), was an early officer.  Women who were awarded the Medal of Excellence in the early years included: Mary Crease Sears, bookbinder; Josephine H. Shaw and Margaret Rogers, jewelers; Sister Magdalen, Winifred Crawford, and Beatrix Holmes, illuminators; Lydia Bush-Brown, batik dyer; and Louise Chrimes, needleworker.

BB12: Guild of Boston Artists

162 Newbury Street

In addition to the art galleries along Newbury Street, many displaying the work of women artists and some owned or managed by women, is the Guild of Boston Artists. It is an association of painters, sculptors, and printmakers founded in 1914. Women have always been active in the guild and were among the charter members. One of its goals is to bring to public attention the work of young greater Boston artists. In addition to its public gallery, the guild sponsors art classes in its building.

Among women members was Bostonian Lilla Cabot Perry (1847-1933), whose paintings are included in the collections of the Museum of Fine Arts and the National Museum of Women in the Arts in Washington, D.C. She studied in Paris and was influenced by Claude Monet. She was his neighbor in Giverny for ten summers, beginning in 1889. Perry also taught and painted in Tokyo for three years. Other Boston women painters include Adelaide Cole Chase (1868-1944), who also studied in Paris and painted still life and portraits, especially of women and children; and painter Gertrude Fiske (1878-1961), who was a founder of the guild and was the first woman named to the Massachusetts Art Commission.

In 1930, Boston sculptor Amelia Peabody (1890-1984) held a major exhibition at the guild. Her sculpture *End of an Era*, depicting the last of the Boston one-horse cabs, was very popular and was acquired by the Museum of Fine Arts. Although she continued to create and exhibit her sculpture, Peabody was also a philanthropist. An ardent sportswoman and lover of animals, especially horses, she provided support to the new Tufts Veterinary School. She divided her time between her home at 120 Commonwealth Avenue and her farm in Dover. Peabody continued creating sculpture late in life, turning to the medium of ceramics. She served on the boards of many Boston hospitals, donating funds—and sculptures—to them.

BB13: The Copley Society of Boston

158 Newbury Street

The oldest art association in America, the Copley Society was founded as the Boston Art Students Association in 1879 by the first graduating class from the Museum School of Boston's Museum of Fine Arts. The founders wanted a place to exhibit the work of young artists and to continue their Museum School associations. The organization changed its name to the Copley Society of Boston in 1901 and membership was no longer restricted to those persons with an affiliation. Sarah Choate Sears (see BB30) and Sarah Wyman Whitman (see BB5) served on the Copley Society's committees. Among other distinguished members were painter Margaret Fitzhugh Brown (1884-1972); Lillian Westcott Hale (1881-1963), known for her carefully drafted charcoal drawings; and Marie Danforth Page (1869-1940), whose portraits often depicted women and children. In addition to showing works by Boston women artists, the Society exhibited paintings by internationally known artists Mary Cassatt (see BB30) and Cecelia Beaux (1855-1942).

Directions: As you walk along Newbury Street to Dartmouth, notice DuBarry's Newbury Street Mural by Joshua Winer, James David Bennette, and Jack Keledjian on the side of the building next to the parking lot. It includes many well-known Boston women including American Revolution-era correspondents Abigail Adams and Mercy Otis Warren, writer Louisa May Alcott, composer Amy Beach, religious leader Mary Baker Eddy, art patron Isabella Stewart Gardner, reformer Julia Ward Howe, scientist Ellen Richards, poet Phillis Wheatley, and sculptor Anne Whitney.

DuBarry's Newbury Street Mural

BB14: Muriel S. Snowden International High School

150 Newbury Street

In 1988, the Boston School Committee renamed Copley Square High School to honor long-time African American community activist, Muriel S. Snowden (1916-1988). With her husband, Otto, Muriel Snowden founded Freedom House, Inc., in Roxbury as a nonprofit community-based organization dedicated to human rights and advocacy for African Americans in Boston. Her leadership moved Freedom House into areas of urban renewal, minority employment, and educational equality for children as well as being a positive force for interracial cooperation in Boston. The high school encourages the study of international cultures and foreign languages, fields Snowden also fostered.

Muriel S. Snowden

Directions: Turn left and walk down Dartmouth Street to Commonwealth Avenue.

BB15: Chilton Club

287 Dartmouth Street at Commonwealth Avenue

The Chilton Club was founded by ten Boston women in 1910 in response to the exclusive men's clubs that did not allow women to be members and, in many cases, to even enter the clubs. The women founders invited 43 other women to become founders and purchased this building as a club house. It is named for Mary Chilton, credited as the first women to step off the Mayflower.

"Freedom House... is an innovator, a catalyst, a launching pad for all kinds of efforts to improve the way of life for those who live in cities... especially the inner core of a city."
—Muriel S. Snowden

Directions: Return to Newbury Street and continue east.

BB16: The School of Fashion Design
136 Newbury Street
The School of Fashion Design was founded in 1934 by Carolyn L. Dewing and Donald Smith-Fedey as the Modern School of Applied Art. In 1936, Dorchester native Isobel Silnesi joined the faculty and was instrumental in adding fashion design to the curriculum. Serving as co-director from 1952 until her death in 1997, Silnesi led the school in developing its curriculum to focus entirely on fashion design.

BB17: Katharine Gibbs School
126 Newbury Street
Katharine Gibbs founded her first business school for women in Providence, Rhode Island, in 1911. She opened a Boston branch six years later. Originally designed to train young women in the new careers in office work that opened up to skilled women at the beginning of the 20th century, the school is now coeducational and offers courses in business administration, accounting, hotel management, paralegal services, and computer science.

Geraldine Field, Ruth Talbot, and Ellen O'Donnell of the Junior League collecting books for the annual campaign for the American Merchant Marine Library Association, 1935

BB18: Junior League of Boston
117 Newbury Street
Boston's Junior League, established in 1907, is the second oldest Junior League in the country. Growing out of the 19th century sewing circle tradition, the league was first known as "The Sewing Circle League." Originally membership was by invitation only among the debutantes of the season. The league soon became interested in the social and industrial problems of the city and changed its name to the Junior League of Boston in 1916. The current Boston League has more than 1,500 members who contribute more than 30,000 hours each year in community service programs. They welcome as members all women who are committed to volunteerism. The League focuses a significant part of its programming on the positive development of adolescent girls and works in collaboration with several organizations with similar goals.

Directions: Note the New England Historic Genealogical Society at 101 Newbury Street. It contains a major library of materials useful in tracing family history and offers regular programs on how to locate female ancestors.

BB19: Church of the Covenant and the Women's Lunch Place

67 Newbury Street

The Church of the Covenant has supported women since they were given the right to vote in all church matters in 1885. Member Abbie Child was the head of the Women's Board of Missions of the Congregational Church in the late 19th century. Member Dr. Elsa Meder was one of the first women ordained to the office of elder in the Presbyterian Church in New England. Elizabeth Rice and Alice Hageman, who were ordained in 1974 and 1975, were the first women to serve as pastors at a Back Bay church. When they were joined by Donna Day Lower, the church became the only one in the United States with three women clergy. The church sanctuary is noted for its Tiffany stained glass windows, including "Four Women of the Bible," portraying Miriam, Deborah, Mary of Bethany, and Dorcas. Since 1982, when Jane Alexander and Eileen Riley opened the Women's Lunch Place, the church has served as a haven for poor women and their children.

BB20: Home of Margaret Deland

35 Newbury Street

Margaret Deland (1857-1945), a turn-of-the-century novelist and social reformer, lived in this house where she welcomed spring with flower boxes of daffodils. Her 25 works of fiction were set both in historical and modern times and dealt with making ethical decisions in different settings. Although she considered herself a "new woman," determined to preserve her own freedom of action, she did not support woman suffrage. Her charity was personal; she took young unwed mothers into her home until they could become self-supporting, believing that their love for their babies would provide an incentive.

Maria Mitchell

BB21: American Academy of Arts and Sciences

28 Newbury Street

Although the American Academy of Arts and Sciences has not occupied this building since 1955 and now is located in Cambridge, its roots are in Boston. Founded during the American Revolution to promote the arts and sciences, it was open only to men until 1943. The exception was astronomer Maria Mitchell (1818-1889), who was elected to the academy in 1848 and for a century held that exclusive position in history. Soon after women were granted suffrage, the academy reconsidered its

"Until women throw off reverence for authority, they will not develop. When they do this...the truth which they get will be theirs and their minds will go on and on, unfettered." —Maria Mitchell

policy of electing only men to its membership. Even though a survey showed 147 members in favor and only 72 opposed, the academy did not elect women until 1943 when it admitted four women including another astronomer, Cecilia Payne-Gaposchkin of Harvard. In 1976 Elma Lewis, the founder of the National Center of Afro-American Artists in Roxbury, was elected to membership (see BB28). Currently about twenty percent of the academy's new members each year are women.

Maria Mitchell was a favorite of 19th-century Boston women, and her annual visit to speak at the New England Women's Club was much celebrated. She grew up on Nantucket, where she learned celestial navigation from her father. In 1847 her discovery of a comet brought her fame and induction into the academy. Mitchell was a strong proponent of women's rights and helped found the Association for the Advancement of Women. She said, "The eye that directs a needle in the delicate meshes of embroidery will equally well bisect a star with the spider web of the micrometer." She also observed that, "Until women throw off reverence for authority, they will not develop. When they do this...the truth which they get will be theirs and their minds will go on and on, unfettered." Mitchell became Vassar College's first woman science professor and director of their observatory. Her observatory and birthplace are maintained by the Maria Mitchell Science Center on Nantucket.

BB22: Leslie Lindsay Chapel, Emmanuel Episcopal Church
15 Newbury Street

The Chapel is a memorial to Leslie Lindsay of Boston, given by her parents. While honeymooning on board the Lusitania, Leslie and her English husband, Stuart Mason, drowned when their ship was torpedoed off the Irish coast by German submarines on May 7, 1915. The Gothic style chapel was completed in 1924.

Directions: Walk to Arlington Street, passing the Ritz-Carlton Hotel. Turn left, and left again on Commonwealth Avenue.

BB23: Home of Amy Beach
28 Commonwealth Avenue

Amy Beach (1867-1944) is one of America's most noted composers. Her work, which has been revived in recent years, is enjoying a new popularity. She began her career as a concert pianist, but after her marriage to Dr. Henry Harris Beach, she turned her talents to composition. When her *Mass in E flat major*, which took three years to complete, was performed by the Handel and Haydn Society with the Boston Symphony Orchestra in February 1892, it was the first work by a woman to be performed by the Society. In the same year her aria for an alto soloist was the first work by a woman to be performed by the New York Symphony Orchestra. Her standing as a

Amy Beach

composer led her to be commissioned to write the *Festival Jubilate* for chorus and orchestra which was played at the dedication of the Woman's Building during Chicago's 1892 World's Columbia Exposition. Beach's *Gaelic Symphony* was performed by orchestras throughout the country. In 1900, she premiered her own piano concerto with the Boston Symphony and later performed it in Europe. In addition to her larger pieces, Beach composed choral works, piano pieces, and over 150 popular songs.

BB24: The College Club
44 Commonwealth Avenue
Founded in 1890, the College Club is the oldest women's college club in the United States. It was founded by nineteen Boston women who were members of the National Association of Collegiate Alumnae (now the American Association of University Women). Their goal was to support higher education for women and to offer members a place to meet. The Club continues to provide scholarships for women.

BB25: Statues and Easter Parade
Commonwealth Avenue Mall
The Commonwealth Avenue Mall is worth exploring as a loop off of the Back Bay Walk. Three of the Mall's statues were created by women: historian Samuel Eliot Morison by Penelope Jencks (near Exeter Street); Argentine president Domingo Sarmiento by Yvette Compagnion (near Gloucester Street); and Norwegian explorer Leif Eriksson by Anne Whitney (see B16) (near Charlesgate). The bust of Boston Mayor Patrick Collins (near Clarendon Street) was created by Theo Ruggles Kitson and her husband, Henry Hudson Kitson. The Collins statue is flanked by two women, one symbolic of Ireland, his birthplace, and the other of America. A women's memorial statue is being planned for the space between Fairfield and Gloucester Streets. Current plans call for it to represent three women: American Revolution-era correspondent Abigail Adams (see D13), suffragist Lucy Stone (see D6), and poet Phillis Wheatley (see C5 and D19).

Julia Oliver O'Neil (1909-1978) and her ten daughters became famous in the Commonwealth Avenue Easter Parade. Every year, between 1940 and 1959, she made matching outfits for her daughters and their picture was printed in journals and newspapers all over the world.

From left to right: Jane, Barbara, Diane, Maureen, Evelyn, Ginny, Mary Jane, Julie, Danielle, Fran, and parents Julia and Dan O'Neil at Boston's Easter Parade in 1953

Directions: If you explore the Commonwealth Avenue Mall, return to and continue along Clarendon Street, crossing Commonwealth Avenue. For BB27, return to Commonwealth Avenue.

BB26: Harriet Hemenway and the Massachusetts Audubon Society

273 Clarendon Street (now Hale House)
Hale House, a residential care facility for the elderly, was the home of Harriet Lawrence Hemenway (1858-1960), who in 1896 founded the Massachusetts Audubon Society with her cousin, Minna Hall (1851-1941). They were protesting the slaughter of birds for feathers to ornament women's hats. It was estimated that five million American birds of about 50 species were being killed annually for this purpose. Hemenway and Hall invited groups of women to tea and convinced about 900 of them to give up wearing feathered hats. Their next move was to invite some prominent men to join them to start the Audubon Society with a goal of protecting birds. Although national legislation took a little longer, by 1897 Massachusetts had passed a bill outlawing trade in wild bird feathers.

Directions: Return to Commonwealth Avenue.

BB27: Simmons College Graduate School of Social Work

51 Commonwealth Avenue
The Simmons College Graduate School of Social Work, founded in 1904, was the first school of social work to be affiliated with an institution of higher learning. When Simmons College was established as a women's college in 1899, Henry LeFavour, the first president, explained that the college hoped to prepare young women to earn their own living. Recognizing that the college's goal was controversial, he explained: "Whether society ought to be constituted so that women should not need to earn their own living is a debatable question, but it is evident that the trend of society is now in the other direction." When the college opened, it offered training in household economics, secretarial studies, library science, and general science. The household economics course developed out of the Women's

On the right, the Simmons College Graduate School of Social Work at 51 Commonwealth Avenue. To its left is 49 Commonwealth, the site of the Prince School of Salesmanship in the late 1940s.

Educational and Industrial Union's School of Housekeeping (see BB1). Social work was added next, followed by salesmanship and public health nursing. The salesmanship program—officially, the Prince School of Education for Store Service—also developed out of the Women's Educational and Industrial Union. Founded in 1905 by Lucinda W. Prince (1862-1935), the program became so popular that Prince soon teamed up with Simmons College to offer teacher training courses for her instructors. By 1915, the program was given its own name—the Prince School of Salesmanship— and it was administered jointly by Simmons and the Union. By 1918, Simmons assumed complete responsibility for the school which was located at 49 Commonwealth Avenue (next to the School of Social Work) in the late 1940s. The Simmons College main campus is located on The Fenway. It offers an undergraduate liberal arts program and twelve graduate programs, including the only women's Master of Business Arts program. The MBA program is housed at 409 Commonwealth Avenue.

The School of Social Work building was owned by Isabella Stewart Gardner's father-in-law, John L. Gardner, who willed it to his son George, who gave it to Simmons. He was influenced by his mother, Eliza Endicott Peabody Gardner, whose life-long interest in social work convinced her son that this was the most appropriate use of their family home.

Directions: Turn back (east) on Commonwealth Avenue to Berkeley Street and cross it.

BB28: Emerson College Buildings
21 to 23 Commonwealth Avenue

Emerson College was established as a school of public speaking in 1880. In the early years, most of its graduates became teachers. With the introduction of radio production to its curriculum, Emerson began to expand its offerings to a wide range of courses and experiences in communi-cation. One of its most

Elma Lewis

distinguished graduates is Elma Lewis, a committed community activist. She founded the Elma Lewis School of Fine Arts in Roxbury in 1950 in order to bring arts to the African American community, especially to young people. She expanded her school to become the National Center of Afro-American Artists between 1969 and 1980. Her production of *Black Nativity* by Langston Hughes is still performed in Boston during the Christmas season. Emerson College awarded Elma Lewis an honorary Doctor of Humanities degree in 1968.

BB29: Boston Center for Adult Education

5 Commonwealth Avenue

Founded in 1933, the Boston Center for Adult Education was the first private, nonprofit adult education center in New England. It offers a range of courses in the humanities, arts, sciences, and professional development. One participant whose course at the Center led to a career in poetry was Anne Gray Sexton (1928-1974). At the age of 28 she took John Holmes's poetry workshop. She began writing poetry as mental therapy, but soon became well known. Suffering from mental depression, she once said, "Poetry saved my life." She was awarded the Pulitzer Prize for her collection, *Live or Die*, in 1967. Although she committed suicide, many of her poems call out for life. She said, "I say Live, Live because of the sun,/ the dream, the excitable gift."

Directions: Turn left on Arlington Street.

Regal Lillies, watercolor by
Sarah Choate Sears

BB30: Home of Sarah Choate Sears

One Commonwealth Avenue
(now Harbridge House)

Artist and art collector Sarah Choate Sears (1858-1935) and her husband Joshua Montgomery Sears lived in this Boston mansion in the first decades of the 20th century. A graduate of the School of the Museum of Fine Arts, Sarah Sears painted portraits and still lifes and later took up photography. A supporter of local artists, Sears was the only woman incorporator of the Society of Arts and Crafts (see BB11). She also was active in the work of the Copley Society (see BB13). Sears was a patron of post impressionist painter Maurice Prendergast, and collected paintings by the early moderns and impressionists. Among them was her acquaintance, American-born Mary Cassatt (1845-1926), whose paintings are treasured by museums worldwide.

Directions: Turn left on Marlborough Street and continue to Berkeley Street.

BB31: French Library and Cultural Center

53 Marlborough Street

Originally organized by members of French-American organizations working toward the liberation of France during World War II, the French Library and Cultural Center opened in 1945. Many women have been involved in creating and expanding the library. Led by Belle P. Rand (1869-1956), ten women and men, half French and half Americans, signed the articles of incorporation. Boston sculptor Katharine Lane Weems (1899-1989) donated her mansion to the Library in 1961. Under the leadership of Edna Doriot, an adjacent building was acquired in 1976. The goal of the center is to promote

French language and culture. In addition to maintaining its library and archives, the French Library sponsors a film program, translation services, and cultural programs including a Bastille Day celebration with dancing on Marlborough Street.

Directions: Return to Berkeley Street
and continue to Beacon Street.

BB32: Home of Isabella Stewart Gardner
150 (152) Beacon Street
(now Emerson College Library)

While she lived at this address, Isabella Stewart Gardner (1840-1924) created one of Boston's most notable places, the Gardner Museum, a magnificent Renaissance Palace located in the Fenway. She called it Fenway Court. Opened in 1903, the museum houses a world-renowned permanent art collection. Her goal was to educate and provide pleasure for the public "forever." Gardner first displayed her paintings in this Beacon Street building which, like Fenway Court, was always filled with flowers and where she was the center of a salon of early 20th century artists, musicians, and writers. Considered an eccentric by some and a genius by others, Gardner was known for her independent attitude and support of the talent in others on her own terms. (For Emerson College, see BB28)

BB33: Gibson House Museum
137 Beacon Street

Isabella Stewart Gardner

When Catherine Hammond Gibson (1804-1888) had her home built on Beacon Street in 1860, she was a pioneer in the settlement of the Back Bay which was built on newly-filled land. Her husband, John Gardner Gibson, a sugar merchant, had been lost at sea and so Catherine moved to the house with her son, Charles Hammond Gibson. Charles Gibson's wife, Rosamond Warren Gibson (1846-1934), moved into the mansion in 1871. She had received the traditional education given to upper-class women in her day, learning French and taking dancing lessons from dancing master Lorenzo Papanti. When the Gibson House opened to the public in 1957, Marjorie Drake Ross (1901-1997), a specialist on the decorative arts and author of *The Book of Boston* series, helped to acquire appropriate objects for the Gibson House and directed the cataloging of the collection. Today, museum tours include interpretive stories of life both "upstairs" and "downstairs" in Victorian

"...her people work as they feel she would have wanted them to do and the place must always remain live for that was the idea in the original conception [of Fenway Court] and in the execution of the idea, a living message of beauty in art to each generation."
—Olga Monks,
Isabella Stewart Gardner's niece, in a letter written shortly after Gardner's death in 1924

Gibson House Museum

Boston. The Victorian Society's New England chapter has been based here since 1974. The society is an advocate for historic preservation, and offers walking tours and lectures on the Victorian era.

BB34: Fisher College
118 Beacon Street
Fisher College was founded in 1903 by Myron C. and Edmund H. Fisher to provide business education for women in a two-year program. In 1939 it moved to this site, the former home of Henry and Alice Spaulding King. The building is noted for its elegant features including a marble hanging stairway. The curriculum has been expanded to offer courses in communication, criminal justice, early childhood education, fashion merchandising, and hotel management. Students come from all over the United States and twelve different countries. Except for continuing education programs, the college was open only to women until 1998.

BB35: The Winsor School, Schools for Girls
95-96 Beacon Street at Embankment Road (now Emerson College Student Union)
Boston's tradition of establishing independent schools for girls is reflected in this site. The Winsor School, founded in 1886, was located in various Back Bay sites including this one until it moved to its present location on Pilgrim Road, near Boston's Fenway, in 1910. Founded by Mrs. Francis Brooks in 1886, the school grew rapidly under the direction of her cousin, Mary Pickard Winsor (1880-1950), who served as its headmistress from its founding until 1922. Many of the students in the first class went on to college, fulfilling the school's mission of college preparation for young women.

Several other independent schools for girls began in the Back Bay. The Haskell School for Girls was located on 314 Marlborough Street from 1903 to 1919. Conducted in the tradition of progressive education, the school was founded by Mary Elizabeth Haskell (1873-1964). Haskell was an activist in the Boston community of her day and in addition to running her school, nurtured the education of promising Boston immigrants, including poet Kahlil Gibran. Haskell became the head of The Cambridge School in 1919, which later became the Cambridge School at Weston. The Brimmer and May School, now located in Chestnut Hill, began in the Back Bay. It was made up of a combination of The May School, founded by Mary May at 339 Marlborough Street at the turn of the 20th century, and the Brimmer School, built in 1914 on Brimmer Street, and the Classical School for Girls.

Directions: Continue along Beacon Street where you can join the Beacon Hill Walk at B17 or enter the Public Garden at Charles Street to see Nancy Schön's sculptures of Mrs. Mallard and her ducklings.

End of Walk.

Credits

Title page: courtesy of Susan Wilson.

Page 9: photo by Susan Wilson.

Page 10: courtesy of The Boston Athenæum.

Page 11: top: photo by Susan Wilson; bottom: courtesy of The Bostonian Society/Old State House.

Page 12: courtesy of The Schlesinger Library, Radcliffe College.

Page 13: courtesy of the Fogg Art Museum, Harvard University.

Page 14: top: courtesy of the Christian Science Publishing Society; bottom: courtesy of Dr. John Duff.

Page 15: top: courtesy of The Schlesinger Library, Radcliffe College; bottom: courtesy of the Peabody Essex Museum, Salem, MA.

Page 16: top: courtesy of the Massachusetts Historical Society, Boston; bottom: bequest of Winslow Warren, courtesy of the Museum of Fine Arts, Boston.

Page 17: courtesy of the University of Nebraska.

Page 18: photo by Susan Wilson.

Page 19: top: photo by Susan Wilson; bottom: courtesy of the Perkins School for the Blind.

Page 20: both: courtesy of The Bostonian Society/Old State House.

Page 21: top: photo by Susan Wilson; bottom: courtesy of The Bostonian Society/Old State House.

Page 22: courtesy of The Bostonian Society/Old State House.

Page 23: courtesy of the Frick Art Reference Library, New York.

Page 25: courtesy of Suzanne Spencer-Wood.

Page 26: top: courtesy of the Langone family; bottom: photo by Susan Wilson.

Page 27: top: courtesy of The Bostonian Society/Old State House; bottom: courtesy of the Boston Public Library.

Page 28: top: courtesy of The Schlesinger Library, Radcliffe College; middle: courtesy of the Society for the Preservation of New England Antiquities; bottom: courtesy of Kate Clifford Larson.

Page 29: courtesy of The Schlesinger Library, Radcliffe College.

Page 31: courtesy of The Boston Athenaeum.

Page 32: top: photo by Susan Wilson; bottom: courtesy of the New England School of Law.

Page 33: top: courtesy of the Peabody Essex Museum, Salem, MA; bottom: courtesy of the Boston Public Library.

Page 34: photo by Susan Wilson.

Page 35: photo by Susan Wilson.

Page 36: top: photo by Susan Wilson; bottom: courtesy of Susan Wilson.

Page 37: top: courtesy of the Schomburg Center for Black Culture; bottom: courtesy of *Black Foremothers* by Sterling.

Page 38: courtesy of the Afro American Studies Center, Boston University.

Page 39: photo by Susan Wilson.

Page 40: top: photo by Joanne Ciccarello; bottom: courtesy of Wellesley College Archives.

Page 41: both, courtesy of The Schlesinger Library, Radcliffe College.

Page 43: courtesy of The Schlesinger Library, Radcliffe College.

Page 44: top: courtesy of the Boston Public Library; bottom: courtesy of *The Boston Globe*.

Page 45: courtesy of the Chin family.

Page 46: top: courtesy of the Maryknoll Mission Archives; bottom: courtesy of The Schlesinger Library, Radcliffe College.

Page 47: top: courtesy of Suzanne Spencer-Wood; bottom: photo by Susan Wilson.

Page 48: courtesy of the International Brotherhood of Electrical Workers.

Page 49: photo by Susan Wilson.

Page 51: top: photo by Susan Wilson; bottom: courtesy of the Women's Educational and Industrial Union.

Page 52: top: courtesy of The Schlesinger Library, Radcliffe College; bottom: courtesy of the Boston Public Library.

Page 53: courtesy of the Sophia Smith Collection, Smith College.

Page 54: courtesy of the Cass family.

Page 55: photo by Jeff Johnson.

Page 56: photo by Susan Wilson.

Page 59: top: photo by Susan Wilson; bottom: photo by Judith Sedwick, courtesy of Ben Wallace.

Page 60: courtesy of the Junior League of Boston.

Page 61: courtesy of the Vassar College Library.

Page 62: courtesy of Virginia Eskin.

Page 63: courtesy of Ginny O'Neil.

Page 64: courtesy of the Simmons College Archives, Boston.

Page 65: courtesy of the Boston Public Library.

Page 66: courtesy of the Museum of Fine Arts, Boston.

Page 67: courtesy of the Isabella Stewart Gardner Museum, Boston.

Page 68: photo by Susan Wilson.

Page 70: photo by Joanne Ciccarello.

Full map: 1992 © Bruce Jones Design, Inc.
modifications and individual maps: Bonnie Hurd Smith

At one time Boston was known for its cobblestone streets. While most of them have long since been replaced by modern paving methods, these lucky ones have been preserved on Louisburg Square (see Beacon Hill Walk.)

More About Boston Women
A Selected List

Books

Alcott, Louisa May. *Hospital Sketches*. Bessie Z. Jones, ed., Harvard University Press, 1960.

Blanchard, Paula. *Margaret Fuller: From Transcendentalism to Revolution*. Addison-Wesley, 1987.

Cantarow, Ellen. *Moving the Mountain: Women Working for Social Change* [Florence Luscomb]. Feminist Press, 1980.

Clifford, Deborah. *Mine Eyes Have Seen the Glory: A Biography of Julia Ward Howe*. Little, Brown, 1979.

Cott, Nancy F. *The Bonds of Womanhood: Woman's Sphere in New England, 1780-1835*. Yale University Press, 1977.

Crawford, Deborah. *Four Women in a Violent Time: Anne Hutchinson, Mary Dyer....* Crown, 1970.

Cromwell, Adelaide M. *The Other Brahmins: Boston's Black Upper Class, 1750-1950*. University of Arkansas Press, 1994.

Davidson, Margaret. *Helen Keller's Teacher* [Annie Sullivan]. Scholastic, 1996.

Drachman, Virgina B. *Hospital with a Heart: Women Doctors and the Paradox of Separatism and the New England Hospital, 1862-1969*. Cornell University Press, 1984.

Dublin, Thomas. *Transforming Women's Work: New England Lives in the American Revolution*. Oxford University Press, 1994.

Dykeman, Therese Boos. *American Women Philosophers, 1650-1930: Six Exemplary Thinkers* [Mercy Otis Warren, Judith Sargent Murray, Ednah Dow Cheney]. Edwin Mellon Press, 1993.

Elbert, Sarah. *A Hunger for Home: Louisa May Alcott's Place in American Culture*. Rutgers University Press, 1987.

Fairbanks, Henry G. *Louise Imogen Guiney: Laureate of the Lost*. Magi Books, 1972.

Faxon, Alicia and Moore, Sylvia, eds. *Pilgrims and Pioneers: New England Women in the Arts* [Charlotte Cushman, Harriet Hosmer, Edmonia Lewis, Anne Whitney]. Midmarch Arts Press, 1987.

Freedman, Florence B. *Two Tickets to Freedom: The True Story of Ellen and William Craft, Fugitive Slaves.* B. Bedrick, 1971.

Gibran, Jean and Kahlil. *Kahlil Gibran, His Life and World* [Back Bay women]. Interlink, rev. ed. 1993.

Gill, Gillian. *Mary Baker Eddy.* Perseus Books, 1998.

Goldfarb, Hilliard T. *The Isabella Stewart Gardner Museum: A Companion Guide and History.* Yale University Press, 1995.

Gollaher, David L. *Voice for the Mad: The Life of Dorothea Dix.* Free Press, 1995.

Graham, Shirley. *The Story of Phillis Wheatley.* Julian Messner, 1949.

Hansen, Debra Gold. *Strained Sisterhood: Gender and Class in the Boston Female Anti-Slavery Society.* University of Massachusetts Press, 1993.

Higginbotham, Evelyn Brooks. *Righteous Discontent: The Women's Movement in the Black Baptist Church, 1880-1920.* Harvard University Press, 1993.

Kaufman, Polly Welts. *Boston Women and City School Politics, 1872-1905.* Garland Publishing, Inc., 1994.

Kerr, Andrea Moore. *Lucy Stone: Speaking Out for Equality.* Rutgers University Press, 1992.

Lerner, Gerda. *The Grimke Sisters from South Carolina: Pioneers for Women's Rights and Abolition.* Schocken Books, 1967.

Matson, Molly, ed. *An Independent Woman: The Autobiogrtaphy of Edith Guerrier.* University of Massachusetts Press, 1992.

Merrill, Marlene Deahl, ed. *Growing Up in Boston's Gilded Age: The Journal of Alice Stone Blackwell, 1872-1874.* Yale University Press, 1990.

Norwood, Stephen H. *Labor's Flaming Youth: Telephone Operators and Worker Militancy, 1878-1923.* University of Illinois Press, 1990.

Nylander, Jane C. *Our Own Snug Fireside: Images of the New England Home.* Alfred A. Knopf, 1994.

Pease, Jane L. and Wiliam H. Pease. *Ladies, Women and Wenches: Choice and Constraint in Antebellum Charleston and Boston.* University of North Carolina, 1990.

Porter, Susan, ed. *Women of the Commonwealth: Work, Family, and Social Change in Nineteenth Century Massachusetts.* [Julia Harrington Duff, Emily Greene Balch, Josephine St. Pierre Ruffin] University of Massachusetts Press, 1996.

Richardson, Marilyn, ed. *Maria W. Stewart, America's First Black Woman Political Writer.* Indiana University Press, 1987.

Richmond, Merle. *Phillis Wheatley: Poet.* Chelsea House, 1988.

Roman, Judith A. *Annie Adams Fields: The Spirit of Charles Street.* Indiana University Press, 1990.

Ronda, Bruce. *Elizabeth Palmer Peabody: A Reformer On Her Own Terms.* Harvard Univeristy Press, 1999.

Smith, Bonnie Hurd. *From Gloucester to Philadelphia in 1790: Excerpts from the Letters of Judith Sargent Murray.* Curious Traveller Press and the Judith Sargent Murray Society, 1998.

Van Doren, Carl. *Jane Mecom: Benjamin Franklin's Favorite Sister.* Augustus M. Kelly, 1973.

Williams, Selma R. *Divine Rebel: The Life of Anne Hutchinson.* Holt, Rinehart and Winston, 1981.

Wilson, Susan. *Boston Sites and Insights.* Beacon Press, 1994.

Wilson, Susan. *Garden of Memories: A Guide to Historic Forest Hills.* Forest Hills Educational Trust, 1998.

Articles

Dubrow, Gail Lee. "Claiming Public Space for Women's History in Boston: A Proposal for Preservation, Public Art, and Public Historical Interpretation." *Frontiers* 13 (1992): 111-147.

Emerson, Rev. Dorothy May. "Boston Women Who Worked for Racial Justice: Eliza Lee Cabot Follen, Lydia Maria Francis Child, Maria Weston Chapman, Mary Ashton Rice Livermore, Maria Louise Baldwin, Florida Ruffin Ridley. *Publication of the Unitarian Universalist Women's Heritage Society* (June, 1993).

Gamber, Wendy. "A Precarious Independence: Milliners and Dressmakers in Boston, 1860-1890." *Journal of Women's History* (Spring 1992): 60-87.

Spencer-Wood, Suzanne M. "Feminist Historical Archaeology and the Transformation of American Culture by Domestic Reform Movements, 1840-1925." *Historical Archaeology and the Study of American Culture,* Lu Ann De Cunszo and Bernard L. Herman, eds. University of Tennessee Press, 1996.

Reference

Notable American Women: A Biographical Dictionary.
Vol. 1-3: Edward T. and Janet James, eds., Harvard University Press, 1971. *Vol. 4:* Barbara Sicherman and Carol Hurd Green, eds., Harvard University Press, 1980.

Also published by the Boston Women's Heritage Trail

Women Artists in the Back Bay: A Walking Tour. 2001.

We Will Walk in Her Steps: West Roxbury Women's Heritage Tour. 2001.

Stepping Back: Roxbury Women's History Trail. 1999.

Walk Her Way: A Boston Women's Heritage Trail in the Neighborhood of Charlestown, Massachusetts. 1997.

Voyages of Women: A Walk through the Neighborhood of Roxbury in Boston. 1995.

The South End Women's Heritage Trail. 1994.

Biographies of Twenty Notable Boston Women: A Curriculum Resource. Mary Smoyer, ed. 1993.

Let Me Tell You Her Story: A Walk Through History with the Women of Jamaica Plain. 1992.

Boston-Area Research Resources

The Boston Athenæum
10 1/2 Beacon Street
Boston, MA 02108
617-227-0270

Boston Public Library
666 Boylston Street
Boston, MA 02116
617-536-5400

The Bostonian Society
15 State Street
Boston, MA 02108
617-720-3285

Jewish Women's Archive
68 Harvard Street
Brookline, MA 02146
617-232-2258

Massachusetts Historical Society
1154 Boylston Street
Boston, MA 02215
617-536-1608

Museum of Fine Arts, Boston
465 Huntington Avenue
Boston, MA 02115
617-267-9300

New England Historic Genealogical
 Society (NEHGS)
101 Newbury Street
Boston, MA 02116
617-536-5740

The Schlesinger Library
Radcliffe Institute for Advanced
Study, Harvard College
10 Garden Street
Cambridge, MA 02138
617-495-8647

Society for the Preservation of
 New England Antiquities (SPNEA)
141 Cambridge Street
Boston, MA 02114
617-227-3956

State House Archives
State House, Room 33
Boston, MA 02133
617-727-2816

Unitarian Universalist
 Women's Heritage Society
2 Elm Street
Malden, MA 02148
781-321-3979

Acknowledgements

Our most sincere thanks to: Pamela Greiff of The Boston Athenæum; Donna Baines of *The Boston Globe*; Matt Greif of the Boston National Historical Park; Aarón Schmidt of the Boston Public Library; Doug Southard of The Bostonian Society/Old State House; Charles Sullivan of the Cambridge Historical Commission; Joanne Ciccarello; Sharlene Cochrane, Kate Ohno of The Franklin Papers, Sterling Library, Yale University; Lydia Dufour of the Frick Art Reference Library; Susan M. Olsen of the Isabella Stewart Gardner Museum; Janet Howell of the Junior League of Boston; Kate Clifford Larson; Chris Steele of the Massachusetts Historical Society, Boston; Bill Meikle; Karen L. Otis of the Museum of Fine Arts, Boston; Carolyn Kirdahy of the Museum of Science, Boston; Stephen Dickerman of the New England Holocaust Memorial; Sandy Goldsmith of the New England School of Law; Cynthia Stone of the North Bennet Street Industrial School; Suzanne Spencer-Wood of the Peabody Museum of Archaeology and Ethnology, Harvard University; Paula Richter and Jean Rees of the Peabody Essex Museum, Salem; Marie-Helene Gold of The Schlesinger Library, Radcliffe Institute for Advanced Study, Harvard College; Claire Goodwin of the Simmons College Archives; Lorna Condon of the Society for the Preservation of New England Antiquities; Rev. Dorothy Emerson of the Unitarian Universalist Women's Heritage Society; Wilma Slaight of the Wellesley College Archives; Clara Garcia of the Women's Educational and Industrial Union;

...and to all those who responded to our initial "Request for Nominations" mailing.

The Board of Directors of the Boston Women's Heritage Trail acknowledges, in particular, the generous and ongoing support of the City of Boston, Thomas M. Menino, Mayor, and the Boston Women's Commission; and the Boston Public Schools, Thomas Payzant, Superintendent.

Our Generous Funders

The Boston Athenæum, BankBoston, Boston Public Schools, Sara Campbell, Ltd., Emerson College, Fleet Bank, Massachusetts Foundation for the Humanities (the state program of the National Endowment for the Humanities), A.C. Ratshesky Foundation, Caroline and Sigmund Schott Foundation, and Simmons College.

Index

Boston Women's Heritage Trail
22 Holbrook Street
Boston, MA 02130
617-522-2872
www.bwht.org

A Project of the Boston Public Schools